Victory Over Fear, Sickness, and Defeat

Victory Over Fear, Sickness, and Defeat

Confessing God's Promises in Every Situation

Marcy Di Michele

Without limiting the rights under copyright(s) reserved below, no part of this publication may be reproduced, stored in or introduced into a retrieval system, or transmitted, in any form, or by any means (electronic, mechanical, photocopying, recording, or otherwise) without the prior permission of the publisher and the copyright owner.

The content of this book is provided "AS IS." The Publisher and the Author make no guarantees or warranties as to the accuracy, adequacy or completeness of or results to be obtained from using the content of this book, including any information that can be accessed through hyperlinks or otherwise, and expressly disclaim any warranty expressed or implied, including but not limited to implied warranties of merchantability or fitness for a particular purpose. This limitation of liability shall apply to any claim or cause whatsoever whether such claim or cause arises in contract, tort, or otherwise. In short, you, the reader, are responsible for your choices and the results they bring.

The scanning, uploading, and distributing of this book via the internet or via any other means without the permission of the publisher and copyright owner is illegal and punishable by law. Please purchase only authorized copies, and do not participate in or encourage piracy of copyrighted materials. Your support of the author's rights is appreciated.

Copyright © 2022 by Marcia Di Michele. All rights reserved.

All Scripture quotations, unless otherwise indicated, are taken from the Holy Bible, New International Version®, NIV®. Copyright ©1973, 1978, 1984, 2011 by Biblica, Inc.™ Used by permission of Zondervan. All rights reserved worldwide. www.zondervan.comThe "NIV" and "New International Version" are trademarks registered in the United States Patent and Trademark Office by Biblica, Inc.™

Book design by eBook Prep: www.ebookprep.com
December 2022
ISBN: 978-1-64457-582-6

Rise UP Publications
644 Shrewsbury Commons Ave
Ste 249
Shrewsbury PA 17361
United States of America
www.riseUPpublications.com
Phone: 866-846-5123

Contents

Chapter 1 *There is Freedom*	1
Chapter 2 *True or False*	9
Chapter 3 *The Right Context*	17
Chapter 4 *And God Said*	23
Chapter 5 *It is Written*	33
Chapter 6 *What does your report say?*	39
Chapter 7 *Identity Crisis*	47
Chapter 8 *The Spirit of Fear*	53
Chapter 9 *Does God Send Sickness?*	59
Chapter 10 *Victory over defeat*	67
Chapter 11 *I Can Do All Things*	75
Chapter 12 *A Good Father*	83
Chapter 13 *The Promised Land*	89
Chapter 14 *Overcoming Giants*	97
Chapter 15 *The Blessing of God*	107
Chapter 16 *Is God in Control?*	115
Chapter 17 *A Better Covenant*	125
Chapter 18 *A Good Life*	133

Afterword	141
Memory Verses	145
Acknowledgments	155
About the Author	157

This is for You, Lord, and because of You.

Chapter One

There is Freedom

Following my resignation from the job I had worked for several years, I was floundering and questioning what I should do with my life. My plans and goals were suddenly derailed; I didn't know where to turn; I didn't know how to deal with the trauma I had experienced. Despite my strong faith, my first course of action was not running to God. I felt He was far away, having betrayed me along with the people around me.

For over ten years, I battled depression, fear, and anxiety. I had frequent panic attacks and suicidal thoughts. My state of mind led me to do things I never thought capable of; my rock bottom was the day I sat in my kitchen for three hours with a bottle of painkillers in my hand. I didn't think, or know, freedom was available.

I grew up in church, but I rarely heard mention of depression or mental illness, apart from the need for a demon to be cast out of the sufferer. Because God and I were not on speaking terms, prayer wasn't a solution.

> Now the Lord is the Spirit, and where the Spirit of
> the Lord is, there is freedom.
>
> — 2 Corinthians 3:17

When I finally got the courage to speak to someone, the response was better than expected. They shared their own experience with mental illness and told me I should seek help from a therapist, so I did. I felt better after pouring my heart out to someone, but I quickly realized a listening ear was all they had to offer, and the recommendation of anti-depressants. I was encouraged to start taking medication and assured that, even though I was a Christian, there was nothing wrong with going that route. It wasn't an indication that I lacked faith.

Ultimately, I decided against taking those pills. I didn't feel peace in my spirit, but I certainly felt comfort in knowing I wasn't alone, and other Christians suffered from this issue. Nevertheless, I knew that comforting words could only go so far. I had to get better and talking about it wasn't working.

> "I am leaving you with a gift—peace of mind and
> heart. And the peace I give is a gift the world
> cannot give. So don't be troubled or afraid."
>
> —John 14:27 (NLT)

> Cast all your anxiety on him because he cares for you.
>
> — 1 Peter 5:7

Mental illness is a common problem, and we should be encouraged to speak about it without fear of judgment. In recent years, the church at large has better addressed this vital subject. There's more acknowledgment that mental illness is real. But encouragement and awareness are not cures in themselves. I needed to solve the root of the problem. What the world offers are merely Band-Aid solutions and coping mechanisms.

The way Christians speak about illness tells you what they believe about the healing power of God and the freedom that comes through the Spirit. I'm not saying this comes from a lack of faith. I believe it's from a lack of understanding. I'm not saying it's your fault if you never receive healing; I'm saying God's will is to heal, and we need to receive that truth in our spirits.

The Bible teaches that we each have a measure of faith; not everyone is at the same level.

> "For I say, through the grace given to me, to everyone who is among you, not to think of himself more highly than he ought to think, but to think soberly, as God has dealt to each one a measure of faith."
>
> — Romans 12:3 (NKJV)

The disciples asked Jesus to increase their faith (Luke 17:5), and the Bible teaches that faith is available to all of us. Someone once questioned an old healing preacher saying, "Not everyone has your faith." The preacher responded, "No, but everyone has [access to] my Bible, and that's where I got the faith!"

> Cast your cares on the LORD and he will sustain you; he will never let the righteous be shaken.
>
> — Psalm 55:22

I didn't know God could heal me of depression; I didn't think it was possible. The most I'd ever heard was that God could heal, but we shouldn't expect it; we should learn to cope the best way possible and know that someday when we get to Heaven, all will be well. I lived with the belief that depression was "my cross to bear"; that life was full of mountains and valleys.

I didn't want to "cope" with depression for the rest of my life; I didn't want to endure it or manage it. Although I didn't properly understand sound doctrine, I knew it wasn't normal to live in misery. I knew there had to be an answer.

Depression is not from God; it's not a test, a life lesson, or a form of discipline; depression is straight from the Devil; it's a spirit that belongs back in the pit of Hell where it came from. It doesn't belong to us! Therefore, we should never say "my depression," "my anxiety," or "my mental illness"; it is not ours.

You will never overcome something you don't hate. You have to despise every form of illness, whether mental or physical. You can't embrace it, own it, or tolerate it. This is a truth I did not know about for a long time.

I specifically remember the day it all ended. My best friend had finally had enough of my bellyaching; she wanted to help and be there for me, but she didn't know what to do anymore. She told me I needed to stop speaking words of death because it wasn't helping; it just made me feel worse.

> The tongue can bring death or life; those who love to talk will reap the consequences.
>
> — Proverbs 18:21 (NLT)

I wasn't looking for help; I just wanted to be a victim and make her feel sorry for me. The realization that my closest friend couldn't stand me anymore was the wake-up call I needed!

That night, I closed myself off in my bedroom, knelt at the side of my bed, and cried out to God in a way I hadn't done in years! I told Him I didn't want this anymore; I didn't want to use it as a crutch or an excuse to get sympathy from people; I didn't want to hold on to something I shouldn't have. I was tired of suffering and allowing past trauma to dictate my life. I told the Lord that I believed He could heal me; just as He had set me free from the sin that had bound me a few years earlier, He could also free me of this.

I spoke aloud: the devil that has plagued my mind for too long has to go, in the name of Jesus. I kid you not; everything was different the following morning. I didn't wake up feeling like I had no reason to live; my mind had cleared. My mind was renewed and washed clean. My life has gone upward since that point because I am full of the joy of the Lord.

> But you have filled my heart with more joy than
> when their wheat and wine are everywhere! I will
> lie down and fall asleep in peace because you
> alone, LORD, let me live in safety.
>
> — Psalm 4:7-8 (CEB)

I had to change some habits in my life: I stopped listening to depressing music and started listening to uplifting scriptural praise and worship; I stopped watching certain TV shows and movies and started watching faith-filled preaching; I began to study the Bible; I prayed with fervor; I fasted.

A few weeks later, the Lord spoke to me through His servant, clear as day, to remind me who I was, and what my purpose is. I found my place in the Kingdom of God. Get your hand to the plough. There's no time for depression when you're active. As soon as you start thinking there's no way forward is when depression sets in. God wants to use you, and there is plenty to do for the Lord!

I'm a different person. I decided to hold God to His Word and stand on His promises. I needed to clear out the junk religion I'd been taught and hold fast to what was mine in Christ.

> [...] "Don't be dejected and sad, for the joy of the LORD is your strength!"
>
> — Nehemiah 8:10 (NLT)

As the church, we should never minimize mental health nor ignore it. People are suffering; they need help, but the ultimate answer is not through therapy, medication, or comforting words. Those can only go so far. The power of the Devil must be broken. A spiritual problem requires a spiritual solution, and mental illness is a spiritual problem. It doesn't mean a person is demon-possessed. It is the case for some. But many people are oppressed and bound by a scheme of the enemy intended to destroy them.

In my case, there was oppression over my life. Demonic strongholds and oppressions exist, and we must destroy them with the power of the name of Jesus.

> "Then should not this woman, a daughter of Abraham, whom Satan has kept bound for eighteen long years, be set free on the Sabbath day from what bound her?"
>
> — Luke 13:16

At times, I've questioned whether some ministers fully believe in the Bible they preach. I've seen them primarily turn to any and every man-made solution rather than going directly to our true source. I'm not saying there is nothing in the world's science or technology that can benefit us. Many inventions have aided in advancing the gospel. However, the answers we need are found within Scripture. It must be our first resort. I didn't have a plan B. Either the Word is completely true, or none of it is. If God said it, He will do it. Not half of it, not just in Heaven, but in this life and in the life to come.

> I remain confident of this: I will see the goodness of
> the LORD in the land of the living.
>
> — Psalm 27:13

Once I understood what the Word of God says and understood His good and perfect will for me, things changed. My prayer for everyone reading this is, if you have a mental illness or you know someone who does, understand what Jesus did for us on the cross; He died to break all the power of the enemy off of our lives: sin, sickness, depression, fear, everything! And if Christ died for it, you don't have to live with it!

> For he has rescued us from the kingdom of darkness
> and transferred us into the Kingdom of his dear
> Son, who purchased our freedom and forgave our
> sins.
>
> — Colossians 1:13-14 (NLT)

I can tell you what cures everything ailing the heart of man. I want you to know all about it. It's the life-giving, life-changing power of the Holy Spirit through the salvation of Christ Jesus. Unspeakable joy comes from living in Christ. Joy can only be experienced, not explained.

Marcy Di Michele

> You make known to me the path of life; in your presence, there is fullness of joy; at your right hand are pleasures forevermore.
>
> — Psalm 16:11 (ESV)

The answer is not to pray harder; it's to pray smarter. In other words, know what to pray and how to pray it. It's a re-education, a renewing of your mind, learning to declare your faith, and a choice to change your lifestyle.

There's a joy from God that clears the clouds of depression away for good. You have to choose it, accept it, and believe it. You don't have to live with mental illness; you don't have to suffer anymore. Your healing was purchased on that cross; it's yours! Take it by faith, in Jesus' name.

> He is so rich in kindness and grace that he purchased our freedom with the blood of his Son and forgave our sins.
>
> — Ephesians 1:7 (NLT)

Chapter Two

True or False

I've heard it said, "You can't preach this stuff, you'll get people's hopes up, and they'll be disappointed and disillusioned with God if it doesn't work out!" (They're defeated before even getting started!) I'm sure some Christians will label me a "health and wealth" preacher and dismiss this book outright. Maybe they will call me a "false teacher" or a "heretic." Religious people often take that position regarding anyone with differing doctrines. It's a Pharisaical reaction. But the Bible does instruct how to deal with false teachers.

> For the time will come when people will not put up with sound doctrine. Instead, to suit their own desires, they will gather around them a great number of teachers to say what their itching ears want to hear. They will turn their ears away from the truth and turn aside to myths.
>
> — 2 Timothy 4:3-4

Marcy Di Michele

If you search for Christian content on social media, you will find a lot of material regarding false prophets. You will find videos, articles, and even Facebook groups naming all the false teachers, heretics, and deceivers. There are YouTube accounts dedicated to pointing out everything "wrong" with what a particular minister is preaching.

I understand the intent behind it. The desire is to ensure no one is led astray by false doctrine. It is Biblical to call out false teaching, but our modern idea of what false teaching is has become nothing more than a difference of opinion. If you see a famous preacher speaking about something you disagree with, you will immediately name them a false prophet according to your personal interpretation of Scripture.

Does this mean that everyone has the proper doctrine? Of course not, which is why we rely on the Holy Spirit and the wisdom of God for understanding. Do some ministers make false claims regarding money? Absolutely. Are there Preachers who teach heresy? Yes, there are. However, we cannot allow personal feelings or opinions to be the deciding factor. We must let the Bible guide us in identifying what a false teacher is.

> Dear friends, do not believe every spirit, but test the spirits to see whether they are from God, because many false prophets have gone out into the world. This is how you can recognize the Spirit of God: Every spirit that acknowledges that Jesus Christ has come in the flesh is from God, but every spirit that does not acknowledge Jesus is not from God. This is the spirit of the antichrist, which you have heard is coming and even now is already in the world.
>
> — 1 John 4:1-3

If you question whether someone is a false teacher, pay attention to how they speak of Jesus. Do they teach Jesus is the Son of God, part of the Holy Trinity, and the only way to Heaven? If you hear messages about Jesus being a good example to follow or a good teacher, but he lacks divinity that is a red flag.

> Jesus answered, "I am the way and the truth and the life. No one comes to the Father except through me."
>
> — John 14:6

Are they teaching about the death and resurrection of Christ? Is there an understanding that the sacrifice of Jesus took our place so through Him we could have salvation? Any notion of another way to Heaven or more than one way to the Father is another red flag.

> Then know this, you and all the people of Israel: It is by the name of Jesus Christ of Nazareth, whom you crucified but whom God raised from the dead, that this man stands before you healed. Jesus is 'the stone you builders rejected, which has become the cornerstone.' Salvation is found in no one else, for there is no other name under heaven given to mankind by which we must be saved.
>
> — Acts 4:10-12

Are they preaching about sin and Hell? I played drums for a church that changed the lyrics of a song to remove the word "sin." If a church or minister does not acknowledge the reality of Hell and that sin is what separates us from God, find another church!

If there is no preaching on repentance, it is not the true gospel. If they avoid admitting there is a Hell, they are not preaching the truth. There is a Heaven and a Hell; sin is from the Devil, so we must flee from it. There are multiple warnings in Scripture to not give in to the lust of the flesh or be led astray by impurity and wrongdoing.

> But as he who called you is holy, you also be holy in all your conduct.
>
> — 1 Peter 1:15 (ESV)

> Since we have these promises, beloved, let us cleanse ourselves from every defilement of body and spirit, bringing holiness to completion in the fear of God.
>
> — 2 Corinthians 7:1 (ESV)

Do they address the subject of holiness? Are they teaching that because Jesus already died, then it does not matter how we live? The Bible is explicitly clear: We must live holy and die to our sinful nature. Jesus constantly instructed people to "go and sin no more!" We are saved by God's grace, but that does not mean we should remain bound to sin. Grace is not a license to sin, it is an empowerment by the Spirit to be free from sin.

> Well then, shall we keep on sinning so that God can keep on showing us more and more kindness and forgiveness? Of course not! Should we keep on sinning when we do not have to? For sin's power over us was broken when we became Christians and were baptized to become a part of Jesus Christ; through his death, the power of your

sinful nature was shattered. Your old sin-loving nature was buried with him by baptism when he died; and when God the Father, with glorious power, brought him back to life again.

— Romans 6:1-4 (TLB)

There are warnings in the Bible about false teachers leading people astray but understanding the subject in the correct context will reveal something entirely different from what the anti-prosperity preachers are trying to promote.

"...But beware of the leaven of the Pharisees and Sadducees." Then they understood that He did not say to beware of the leaven of bread, but of the teaching of the Pharisees and Sadducees.

— Matthew 16:11-12 (NASB1995)

The Pharisees were labeled hypocrites because they had an outward religious appearance, but there was no heart transformation. They kept holding to past laws, not understanding why Jesus had come. They viewed their salvation in the light of how well they kept the ceremonial laws rather than repenting and confessing Jesus as Lord.

Paul addresses a similar issue in Acts 20, where he warns the people about wolves in sheep's clothing. These "wolves" told the Gentiles they must keep the customs of Jewish ceremonial laws to receive salvation.

Keep watch over yourselves and all the flock of which the Holy Spirit has made you overseers. Be shepherds of the church of God, which he bought with his own blood. I know that after I leave,

> savage wolves will come in among you and will not spare the flock. Even from your own number men will arise and distort the truth in order to draw away disciples after them. So be on your guard!...
>
> — Acts 20:28-31

> Religious tradition has distorted the gospel, which is grace through faith in Christ Jesus.
> For it is by grace you have been saved, through faith —and this is not from yourselves, it is the gift of God, not by works, so that no one can boast.
>
> — Ephesians 2:8-9

Salvation does not come by obeying the law solely. Paul was concerned that the Judeans, who did not believe Jesus was the Messiah, would swoop in once he left and lead people astray.

> Now He could do no mighty work there, except that He laid His hands on a few sick people and healed them. And He marveled because of their unbelief.
>
> — Mark 6:5-6 (NKJV)

There is a danger of falling into the trap of unbelief by following preachers who teach about the love of God but then strip Him of His power. You cannot grasp the entirety of whom God is without understanding His power, the power of the Holy Spirit, and the anointing that we receive. Take God at His Word, especially when it comes to giving and healing. If you are grounded in God's truth, it is not possible to have "too much faith."

> When Jesus heard this, he marveled and said to those who followed him, "Truly, I tell you, with no one in Israel have I found such faith."
>
> — Matthew 8:10 (ESV)

> You unbelieving and perverse generation," Jesus replied, "how long shall I stay with you and put up with you? Bring your son here."
>
> — Luke 9:41

Jesus marveled at great faith, and rebuked unbelief.

If you're told you have too much faith, you're talking to the wrong person! It's impossible to please God without faith. Doubt is a form of atheism. When you doubt God's Word, you doubt He exists! [Jesse Duplantis].

So, if we please God by our faith, how can we be sure we believe in the correct promises? Sound doctrine is so important in the life of a Christian!

Is it heresy to claim the promises of God over your life? Are they for New Testament Christians?

> Know therefore that the Lord your God is God; He is the faithful God, keeping His covenant to a thousand generations of those who love Him and keep His commands.
>
> — Deuteronomy 7:9

Is that just for the people of Israel?

> In the same way, "Abraham believed God, and God

> counted him as righteous because of his faith." The real children of Abraham, then, are those who put their faith in God. What's more, the Scriptures looked forward to this time when God would make the Gentiles right in his sight because of their faith. God proclaimed this good news to Abraham long ago when he said, "All nations will be blessed through you." So all who put their faith in Christ share the same blessing Abraham received because of his faith.
>
> — Galatians 3:6-9 (NLT)

> And now that you belong to Christ, you are the true children of Abraham. You are his heirs, and God's promise to Abraham belongs to you.
>
> — Galatians 3:29 (NLT)

If we have received salvation, we are children of God through faith in Christ Jesus, and the same promises given to Abraham, Isaac, and Jacob belong to us!

If God says I can walk in divine health, I will take it seriously. If God says He wants to prosper me, I will believe it. All the answers we need are in the pages of the Bible. Therefore, you must be careful whom you label a false prophet; it is a heavy accusation. If they teach something false, God will hold them accountable. Learn correct doctrine and speak correct doctrine. Personal opinions aren't welcome!

Chapter Three

The Right Context

The biggest challenge Christians face in their study of the Bible is how to apply the Scriptures to their lives and whether there is an application at all. How can we know if a promise is for us or simply for the original audience? When we read the Bible, we must read it for what it says and not what we think it says or want it to say.

The study of Hermeneutics (the science of Biblical interpretation) will greatly aid us in discovering how a particular Scripture applies to us today. We should ask ourselves these basic questions:

1. What did the text mean to the original author and his audience?
2. What is the immediate context of the passage under consideration?
3. What is the specific historical-cultural context and purpose of this book? [1]

The debate on Biblical context rages on in Christian circles because so much contrasting information is available at our fingertips. Additionally, we all have an inherent bias regarding Biblical interpretation, based on our upbringing and experiences. That bias often shapes how we view Scripture, even if it is incorrect.

Therefore, the solution is simple: To know the meaning of a passage, we need to understand it in the proper context, and then we can assess the appropriate application. We will use an oft-debated verse as an example:

> "For I know the plans I have for you," declares the Lord, "plans to prosper you and not to harm you, plans to give you hope and a future."
>
> — Jeremiah 29:11

The purpose of the book of Jeremiah can be broken down into three sections:

1. Historically: To give the history of the last five kings of the House of Judah, the destruction of the temple, the desolation of the city, and the captivity of the nation in Babylon.
2. Spiritually: To show God's grace and mercy in calling a backslidden nation to return to the Lord.
3. Prophetically: To predict the destiny of the chosen nation and the Gentile nations. [2]

Jeremiah's prophecies were directed to the people of Judah and the discouraged and dismayed people scattered around the land of Palestine.[3] The verse in question was spoken as a consolation that a faithful remnant would return after seventy years.[4]

Once we have established the immediate context of the verse, we then must establish whether it is a timeless truth or a culturally specific application. We have to determine whether the book's larger context limits the application or promotes universal application. And finally, is the passage "contradicted" somewhere else to show that it is limited to exceptional situations? [5]

This is where we view a passage in light of the weight of Scripture. In other words, is the truth and/or lesson repeated elsewhere? Is it a consistent theology throughout Scripture, or is it isolated for a particular and exclusive purpose?

In this case, what does God say about having plans for His people in the entirety of the Bible? What does He say about prosperity, hope, and the future?

> I will instruct you and teach you in the way you should go; I will counsel you with my loving eye on you.
>
> — Psalm 32:8

> Trust in the LORD with all your heart and lean not on your own understanding; in all your ways submit to him, and he will make your paths straight.
>
> — Proverbs 3:5-6

> Beloved, I pray that you may prosper in all things and be in health, just as your soul prospers.
>
> — 3 John 2 (NKJV)

> This book of the law shall not depart out of thy mouth; but thou shalt meditate therein day and night, that thou mayest observe to do according to all that is written therein: for then thou shalt

make thy way prosperous, and then thou shalt have good success.

— Joshua 1:8 (KJV)

He shall be like a tree planted by the rivers of water, that brings forth its fruit in its season, whose leaf also shall not wither; and whatsoever he does shall prosper.

— Psalm 1:3 (NKJV)

Praise the LORD! Blessed is the man who fears the LORD, who delights greatly in His commandments. His descendants will be mighty on earth; the generation of the upright will be blessed. Wealth and riches will be in his house, and his righteousness endures forever.

— Psalm 112:1-3 (NKJV)

The thief comes only to steal and kill and destroy. I came that they may have life and have it abundantly.

— John 10:10 (ESV)

But seek first his kingdom and his righteousness, and all these things will be given to you as well.

— Matthew 6:33

We know that Jeremiah 29:11 encourages the captives in Babylon. Nevertheless, it would be irresponsible to claim that we should not believe God wants to prosper us also or that we do not have a hope of a great future. We understand who the original audience was. But the timeless application of that truth is found everywhere throughout the Bible, both in the Old and New Testaments.

Why is it important to understand that verse in context? Because if you believe God only had a good future in mind for the captives in Babylon, you will likely accept defeat and turmoil in your own life. You might even feel there is no point pressing in with prayer because you should not expect things to turn around or get better. And worst of all, your understanding of God's nature and intentions towards us will be misguided.

I used to have that misunderstanding. Why would I believe everything is going to work out for me? Why would I believe that there is prosperity on this side of eternity? I lived life in constant discouragement, struggle, and helplessness, simply waiting for Heaven. Too many Christians live that same way.

The Apostle Paul dealt with more intense persecution and hardship than nearly anyone else. But the last thing we read about him in the book of Acts is that "He proclaimed the kingdom of God and taught about the Lord Jesus Christ—with all boldness and without hindrance!" – Acts 28:31

Remember, your prayers cannot be aligned against God's Word and the prophecy it contains. You must pray in line with God's will. Instead of trying to get God to anoint what you would like to happen, figure out what God wants, and ask Him to anoint you to carry out His purposes.

> But the Lord stood at my side and gave me strength, so that through me the message might be fully proclaimed and all the Gentiles might hear it. And I was delivered from the lion's mouth. The Lord will rescue me from every evil attack and will bring me safely to his heavenly kingdom. To him be glory for ever and ever. Amen.
>
> — 2 TIMOTHY 4:17-18

If Paul still found success after everything he had been through, do you think there is no hope for you? God had a plan for Paul's life, He has a plan for your life, and it is a good plan!

---

[1] Henry A. Virkler, Hermeneutics: Principles and Processes of Biblical Interpretation (Grand Rapids, MI: Baker Publishing Group, 2007), 82

[2] Kevin J. Conner, Old Testament Survey (Portland, OR: City Bible Publishing, 1975)

[3] Norman L. Geisler, A Popular Survey of the Old Testament (Grand Rapids, MI: Baker Publishing Group, 1977), 266

[4] Norman L. Heisler, A Popular Survey of the Old Testament (Grand Rapids, MI: Baker Publishing Group, 1977), 267

[5] Norman L. Geisler, A Popular Survey of the Old Testament (Grand Rapids, MI: Baker Publishing Group, 1977), 266

Chapter Four

And God Said

> Death and life are in the power of the tongue, and
> those who love it will eat its fruits.
>
> — Proverbs 18:21 (ESV)

The Bible begins with the account of God creating the earth. He did not form it with His hands, build it with material, or draw it; He spoke it into existence. The first thing God intended us to learn was the power of words. Eight verses in Genesis chapter 1 start with the phrase, "And God said." His words created life, and just as words build up, they can tear down.

Marcy Di Michele

> [...] no human being can tame the tongue. It is a restless evil, full of deadly poison. With the tongue we praise our Lord and Father, and with it we curse human beings, who have been made in God's likeness. Out of the same mouth come praise and cursing. My brothers and sisters, this should not be.
>
> —James 3:8-10

Although James highlighted the difficulty in controlling our words, humanly speaking, we know that submitting our lives to the Spirit of God will influence what we say.

> The mind governed by the flesh is death, but the mind governed by the Spirit is life and peace.
>
> —Romans 8:6

The strength of the Spirit gives us the ability to restrain wrong words from coming out of our mouths. If we are governed by the Spirit, our words and actions will spring out from a desire to please Him.

> A good man brings good things out of the good stored up in his heart, and an evil man brings evil things out of the evil stored up in his heart. For the mouth speaks what the heart is full of.
>
> —Luke 6:45

Peter, in his first book, quoted this Scripture from Psalm 34.

> For, whoever would love life and see good days must

> keep their tongue from evil and their lips from deceitful speech. They must turn from evil and do good; they must seek peace and pursue it. For the eyes of the Lord are on the righteous and his ears are attentive to their prayer, but the face of the Lord is against those who do evil.
>
> — 1 Peter 3:10-12

From this passage, we find the instructions necessary to achieve the promise. We must guard what we say. The promises of God are true and will always happen, but they also come with conditions connected to obedience. God's promises are a guarantee for those who obey His commands.

If our words were not important, salvation would not require confession. If you do not believe in your heart, it is an empty confession. The words you speak confirm what you believe. Your heart and words have to be tied together to produce a result. A heart belief and verbal confession go hand in hand.

If your significant other declares their love for you and you stand there smiling without saying anything, you will probably be out of the relationship very quickly. Knowing something in your heart is only half the battle. Your words have to confirm it. The Bible shows us that our words carry both good and bad consequences.

> That if you confess with your mouth Jesus as Lord, and believe in your heart that God raised Him from the dead, you will be saved; for with the heart a person believes, resulting in righteousness, and with the mouth he confesses, resulting in salvation.
>
> — Romans 10:9-10 (NASB)

> If we confess our sins, He is faithful and righteous, so that He will forgive us our sins and cleanse us from all unrighteousness.
>
> — 1 John 1:9 (NASB)

> But what does it say? "The word is near you, in your mouth and in your heart" (that is, the word of faith that we proclaim).
>
> — Romans 10:8 (ESV)

When the 12 spies explored the Promised Land, only two returned with a positive report (Joshua and Caleb), and 10 returned with a negative one.

> But because my servant Caleb has a different spirit and follows me wholeheartedly, I will bring him into the land he went to, and his descendants will inherit it.
>
> — Numbers 14:24

The spies with the positive report received honor and success. What about the rest of them?

> So the men Moses had sent to explore the land, who returned and made the whole community grumble against him by spreading a bad report about it—these men who were responsible for spreading the bad report about the land were struck down and died of a plague before the Lord.
>
> — Numbers 14:36-37

All the disciples witnessed Jesus appearing to them after the resurrection, but only one spoke doubt and received a rebuke for his lack of faith. In fact, his nickname, doubting Thomas, is essentially the only thing we know about him and associate with him. I do not know about you, but I would not want to be known as a doubter until the end of time!

> Then Jesus told him, "Because you have seen me, you have believed; blessed are those who have not seen and yet have believed."
>
> —John 20:29

In the book of Acts, we read the account of Ananias and Sapphira, who robbed God with their offerings. After her husband died, Sapphira had a chance to confess. Instead, she lied and was struck dead, just like Ananias. Committing the offense was not what killed her but rather what she said about it.

> About three hours later, his wife came in, not knowing what had happened. Peter asked her, "Tell me, is this the price you and Ananias got for the land?" "Yes," she said, "that is the price." Peter said to her, "How could you conspire to test the Spirit of the Lord? Listen! The feet of the men who buried your husband are at the door, and they will carry you out also." At that moment, she fell down at his feet and died. [...]
>
> —Acts 5:7-10

Esther's decision to approach the King was a risk, but look at what Mordecai reminded her of in chapter 4, verse 14: "For if you remain silent at this time, relief and deliverance for the Jews will arise from another place, but you and your father's family will perish. And who knows but that you have come to your royal position for such a time as this?"

What happened as a result? She saved an entire nation of people while his own gallows hanged her enemy, Haman, further proving the truth found in Proverbs 12:6 "The words of the wicked lie in wait for blood, but the speech of the upright rescues them."

King Nebuchadnezzar attempted to trap Shadrach, Meshach, and Abednego by asking them, "What god will be able to rescue you from my hand?" (Daniel 3:15). Their response was one of faith. "If we are thrown into the blazing furnace, the God we serve is able to deliver us from it, and he will deliver us from Your Majesty's hand." (Daniel 3:17). Imagine if they grumbled to themselves, "How are we going to get out of this one? We're doomed!" No, they chose to speak faith and truth, despite the risk of the fiery furnace.

Our great example, Jesus, consistently displayed and taught the value and importance of speaking.

> "But I tell you that everyone will have to give account on the day of judgment for every empty word they have spoken. For by your words you will be acquitted, and by your words you will be condemned."
>
> — Matthew 12:36-37

When Jesus healed the man at the pool of Bethesda, He did not pick him up and put him into the water. He did not just touch him and stay silent. He spoke to him, and the man received his healing.

> Then Jesus said to him, "Get up! Pick up your mat and walk." At once the man was cured; he picked up his mat and walked. [...]
>
> — John 5:8-9

In Mark 11:23 (ESV), Jesus gives an unusual promise to his disciples. "Truly, I say to you, whoever says to this mountain, 'Be taken up and thrown into the sea,' and does not doubt in his heart, but believes that what he says will come to pass, it will be done for him."

Here, faith without doubt is the condition to meet if one wants the fulfillment of the benefits. The promise is that everyone who meets the condition will be answered, even to the moving of mountains. Everyone, without exception, is promised everything he asks for in prayer, provided he qualifies for an answer.[1]

What are the conditions for answered prayer?

1. Have faith in God.
2. Say, in no uncertain terms, what you want.
3. Have unlimited faith without limiting God's will.
4. Refuse to doubt in your heart.
5. Believe that whatever is asked will be given.
6. Believe that whatever is asked is already granted.
7. Be authoritative and command that what is asked will come to pass.
8. Believe that what you want is God's will.
9. Never say "if it be Thy will" concerning anything you ask, as it is definitely promised of God in His Word.
10. Have a clean heart and life with God and man.[2]

In Mark 4:39 (NKJV), Jesus demonstrated the power of speaking when He addressed the storm. "Then He arose and rebuked the wind, and said to the sea, "Peace, be still!" And the wind ceased and there was a great calm." It was an important demonstration of Jesus rebuking the Devil and his work.

Who caused the squall? If God, then Jesus rebuked God and His work, but if Satan, then all is clear. Satan is the prince of the power of the air and can cause storms with the permission of God.[3]

The storm would not have stopped if Jesus simply stood up, faced the storm, and thought positive thoughts; the command had to come out of His mouth. We find another such occurrence in Luke 4:35 (ESV) when Jesus rebuked a demon spirit. "But Jesus rebuked him, saying, "Be silent and come out of him!" And when the demon had thrown him down in their midst, he came out of him, having done him no harm."

In a similar fashion to the storm, a word of rebuke solved the problem. A sincere heart did not get the job done. The ministry of Jesus taught us a powerful lesson: faith and speaking go hand in hand. Know what to say, how to pray, and how to believe. And that comes with the knowledge of God's Word, and His Word is His will.

Christians today can expect to apply the Gospel's miracle stories by praying for similar manifestations of God's power in Jesus' name, to demonstrate His deity and His superiority over all other objects of worship.[4]

As we read earlier in this chapter, we see the Bible says that faith comes by hearing the Word of God. When you speak and declare the promises of God and the truths of His Word aloud, you hear what you are saying, and it builds your faith. A surefire way to do this in any area of your life is to speak out what the Word says about it.

We are not moved by what we see; we are moved by what the Word of God says. And His Word does not change based on your circumstances. James was killed in Acts chapter 12, and Peter was prepared for the same fate, but when the church prayed, he was broken out of prison.

> So Peter was kept in prison, but the church was earnestly praying to God for him.
>
> — Acts 12:5

Faith does not hope something will happen; faith calls it done. The finished work on the cross is everything we need. It is yours to receive! Faith does not deny reality; faith is the assurance of things not yet seen. So maybe you do not yet see an answer in the natural, but faith is the confidence that, in the supernatural, it is already finished.

I do not have to fake being positive; I do not have to try hard to speak positive things. I have a Wellspring of the river of Life that flows within me. Jesus lives in my heart. The Word of God bubbles up inside me, gives me strength, and sharpens me like a double-edged sword. Just like my favorite Evangelist always says: "You're not wrong when you quote God."

---

[1] Finis Jennings Dake, Dake's Annotated Reference Bible (Lawrenceville, GA: Dake Publishing Inc, 2014), 84

[2] Finis Jennings Dake, Sake's Annotated Reference Bible (Lawrenceville, GA: Dake Publishing Inc, 2014), 97

[3] Finis Jennings Dake, Dake's Annotated Reference Bible (Lawrenceville, GA: Dake Publishing Inc, 2014), 69

[4] William W. Klein, Introduction to Biblical Interpretation (Word Publishing, 1993), 342

Chapter Five

It is Written

> It is written: "I believed; therefore I have spoken." Since we have that same spirit of faith, we also believe and therefore speak.
>
> — *2 CORINTHIANS 4:13*

In Matthew chapter 3, Jesus was baptized in water and the Holy Spirit. The timing is significant because it gives us a better understanding of how we can handle opposition from the enemy. The infilling of the Holy Spirit is a prerequisite for overcoming faith. The next thing we read about Jesus is that the Devil came to tempt Him after He had finished fasting.

> Then Jesus was led by the Spirit into the wilderness to be tempted by the devil. After fasting forty days and forty nights, he was hungry. The tempter came to him and said, "If you are the Son of God, tell these stones to become bread." Jesus answered, "It is written: 'Man shall not live on

> bread alone, but on every word that comes from the mouth of God.'"
>
> — Matthew 4:1-4

Jesus was referencing Deuteronomy 8:3 (NASB): [...] man shall not live on bread alone, but man shall live on everything that comes out of the mouth of the LORD.

> Then the devil took him to the holy city and had him stand on the highest point of the temple. "If you are the Son of God," he said, "throw yourself down. For it is written: 'He will command his angels concerning you, and they will lift you up in their hands, so that you will not strike your foot against a stone.'"
>
> — Matthew 4:5-6

Here, the Devil was quoting Psalm 91:11-12 which says, "For he will command his angels concerning you to guard you in all your ways; they will lift you up in their hands, so that you will not strike your foot against a stone."

Matthew 4:7 goes on to say: Jesus answered him, "It is also written: 'Do not put the Lord your God to the test.'" Here, Jesus was referencing Deuteronomy 6:16: "Do not put the LORD your God to the test as you did at Massah."

> Again, the devil took him to a very high mountain and showed him all the kingdoms of the world and their splendor. "All this I will give you," he said, "if you will bow down and worship me." Jesus said to him, "Away from me, Satan! For it is

> written: 'Worship the Lord your God, and serve him only.' Then the devil left him, and angels came and attended him.
>
> — Matthew 4:8-11

Jesus quoted Deuteronomy 6:13: "Fear the LORD your God, serve him only and take your oaths in his name."

Jesus was ready to take on the Devil in the wilderness. He had been filled with the Spirit and empowered by fasting and prayer. He had an intimate knowledge of the Word of God. The Devil knows the Word too, and he tried to use it against Jesus. Even today, people can use the Bible as a weapon in the wrong sense and in the wrong context. It can lead others astray and cause damage and division.

> Finally, be strong in the Lord and in his mighty power. Put on the full armor of God, so that you can take your stand against the devil's schemes. For our struggle is not against flesh and blood, but against the rulers, against the authorities, against the powers of this dark world and against the spiritual forces of evil in the heavenly realms. Therefore, put on the full armor of God, so that when the day of evil comes, you may be able to stand your ground, and after you have done everything, to stand. Stand firm then, with the belt of truth buckled around your waist, with the breastplate of righteousness in place, and with your feet fitted with the readiness that comes from the gospel of peace. In addition to all this, take up the shield of faith, with which you can extinguish all the flaming arrows of the evil one. Take the helmet of salva-

> tion and the sword of the Spirit, which is the word of God.
>
> — Ephesians 6:10-17

This timeless Scripture describes the armor we are to put on to combat the Devil's schemes. God does not expect us to go into battle ill-prepared or empty-handed. He has given us everything we need to overcome. We must pick up that armor, put it on, and take our stand.

If we use the Word incorrectly, it will not work, just like the Devil did. He quoted an important truth in Psalm 91; however, the context in which he used it was in error. That Scripture does not mean we should purposely put ourselves in danger for no reason. It means we can trust God to protect us from evil, sickness, and harm when we live in obedience to Him.

Jesus understood the context of Scripture, and every time He used it correctly, the Devil was forced to change the subject. He was no match for the power of God's Word.

Remember this: the Devil is not God's evil twin; he is a created being who rebelled against God. The Devil is under the feet of Jesus; therefore, because we are His body, he is under our feet too! It is not a fair fight, and you have the upper hand. The victory was already won when Jesus died and rose again, so there is no circumstance where the Devil has any advantage over you.

We are not sitting ducks, waiting for the Devil to take us out. He cannot destroy a child of God who understands who they are; that is the key. We must understand who we are in Christ and the power available to us.

I remember living in an apartment, and the cable I had on my TV was from my property owner. Back then, there was no on-screen guide, so the only way to know what channels you had was to flip through all of them. I thought it was just a basic cable package, but one day, a friend came over and discovered a plethora of channels I did not know I had. They were all available to me, but I never took the time to check. That is the case with many Christians; God makes so much available to us, but we do not know to tap into it.

> My people are destroyed for lack of knowledge;
> because you have rejected knowledge, I reject you
> from being a priest to me. And since you have
> forgotten the law of your God, I also will forget
> your children.
>
> — Hosea 4:6 (ESV)

We must know what the Word of God says, especially what it says about us. Do not be held back by a lack of understanding. You will never rise higher than what you believe, and you will never rise higher than what you say.

While you are on this earth, you will face opposition. But the Bible says...

> For every child of God defeats this evil world, and we
> achieve this victory through our faith. And who
> can win this battle against the world? Only those
> who believe that Jesus is the Son of God.
> And we are confident that he hears us whenever we
> ask for anything that pleases him. And since we
> know he hears us when we make our requests, we
> also know that he will give us what we ask for.
>
> — 1 John 5:4-5, 14-15 (NLT)

The Word of God is powerful when you believe it and speak it. Many people hear what the Devil is doing and repeat it out of their mouths, almost like a reflex. And when you constantly speak negatively, you feel negative. When we speak doubt, fear, discouragement, gossip, and negativity, we are opening the door to demonic strongholds in our lives. The Devil does not have to do much, he just plants a seed, and we take care of his work for him.

In Genesis 3, the serpent went to Eve, and the first thing he spoke was doubt, by questioning what God said. When Eve repeated the command, the Devil challenged its validity. In Genesis 2, when God gave the command to Adam about the tree of good and evil, Eve was not yet created. We see no account of God repeating it to Eve, so we can assume Adam told her. Perhaps that is why the serpent approached Eve instead of Adam.

> Now the serpent was more crafty than any other beast of the field that the LORD God had made. He said to the woman, "Did God actually say, 'You shall not eat of any tree in the garden?'"
>
> — Genesis 3:1 (ESV)

Rather than use God's Word as a powerful weapon, Eve succumbed to the Devil's trickery. Adam, who was with her the whole time, never spoke up. He knew what was right in his heart, but he was silent in the face of the challenge. The rest is history.

Chapter Six

What does your report say?

We have to guard our confession. Never allow doubt or wavering to come out of your mouth. Since we have established that we are sons and daughters of Abraham through faith in Christ Jesus, we should look to him for instructions on how to believe. After all, God hand selected Abram to build a nation.

> The Lord had said to Abram, "Go from your country, your people and your father's household to the land I will show you. "I will make you into a great nation, and I will bless you;
> I will make your name great, and you will be a blessing. I will bless those who bless you, and whoever curses you I will curse; and all peoples on earth will be blessed through you.
>
> — Genesis 12:1-3

When God said go, Abram went. When God gave a command, he followed it. He didn't take time to pray or think about it; he didn't consult with his wife or his servants. He obeyed God's instructions.

> Without weakening in his faith, he faced the fact that his body was as good as dead—since he was about a hundred years old—and that Sarah's womb was also dead. Yet he did not waver through unbelief regarding the promise of God but was strengthened in his faith and gave glory to God, being fully persuaded that God had the power to do what he had promised. This is why "it was credited to him as righteousness.
>
> — Romans 4:19-22

What an amazing legacy! Abraham never wavered. He did not have unbelief regarding the promises of God. He didn't have Jesus. The Holy Spirit wasn't poured out. Yet, his faith was strong. He believed God, and took Him at His word.

Although we benefit from the entirety of Scripture, we are tainted by disappointment. Our forefathers had a pure faith. They didn't see failure. We, on the other hand, are surrounded by bad news, sad stories, and bitter people. It takes a complete change in perspective to look solely to the Bible, and not be swayed by circumstances or experiences.

When I wrote this book, the world was facing threats of food shortages, rising gas prices, and multiple plagues.

Let me ask you this: how did Isaac handle a time of famine?

> The Lord appeared to Isaac and said, "Do not go down to Egypt; live in the land where I tell you to

> live. Stay in this land for a while, and I will be
> with you and will bless you. For to you and your
> descendants I will give all these lands and will
> confirm the oath I swore to your father Abraham.
> I will make your descendants as numerous as the
> stars in the sky and will give them all these lands,
> and through your offspring all nations on earth
> will be blessed, because Abraham obeyed me and
> did everything I required of him, keeping my
> commands, my decrees and my instructions." So
> Isaac stayed in Gerar.
>
> — Genesis 26:2-6

Isaac received instruction from God, and he followed it. It's so important to know the Word, and speak the Word. God told Isaac what to do, and He reminded Isaac of the promises. There's no excuse for not knowing. The more you read and speak, the more you remember. Allow the promises of God to drown out the voice of the enemy.

> Isaac planted crops in that land and the same year
> reaped a hundredfold, because the Lord blessed
> him. The man became rich, and his wealth
> continued to grow until he became very wealthy.
> He had so many flocks and herds and servants
> that the Philistines envied him.
>
> — Genesis 26:12-14.

Isaac sowed during a famine and became very rich as a result. He prospered when others suffered and became the envy of his enemies. What is your response to a challenge in the world? Do you communicate doubt and worry, or do you follow the Lord's leading?

Marcy Di Michele

Do you regurgitate what those around you say, or do you remind yourself of the Scripture?

> In my distress I prayed to the Lord, and the Lord answered me and set me free. The Lord is for me, so I will have no fear. What can mere people do to me? Yes, the Lord is for me; he will help me. I will look in triumph at those who hate me. It is better to take refuge in the Lord than to trust in people. It is better to take refuge in the Lord than to trust in princes. Though hostile nations surrounded me, I destroyed them all with the authority of the Lord. Yes, they surrounded and attacked me, but I destroyed them all with the authority of the Lord.
>
> — Psalm 118:5-10 (NLT)

Say this aloud: I will not fear. I have the victory. I carry the authority of the Lord. I trust in Him.

That's how we are to carry ourselves. Take the posture of an overcomer.

> Once I was young, and now I am old. Yet I have never seen the godly abandoned or their children begging for bread.
>
> — Psalm 37:25 (NLT)

I will never be in lack. My family will never be in lack. I will not go without.

What does your report say? Does it speak doubt, or does it speak faith? Does it speak hopelessness, or does it speak confidence?

> I remain confident of this: I will see the goodness of the Lord in the land of the living. Wait for the Lord; be strong and take heart and wait for the Lord.
>
> — Psalm 27:13-14

God cannot fail. It's not in His nature. He is our rescuer, our protector, our provider, and our sustainer. We don't look to any man to be our source. Our source is the Lord, the maker of Heaven and earth. Our God in whom we trust. What is there to be afraid of?

> Submit yourselves therefore to God. Resist the devil, and he will flee from you.
>
> — James 4:7 (ESV)

This verse requires two key elements to see the Devil flee from us:

1 - to submit to God, and
2 - to resist the Devil.

The original Greek defines the word 'submit' in this Scripture as: "to rank under, to be placed in subjection to; to obey; to absolutely yield to advice." The original Greek defines the word 'resist' to mean: "oppose, withstand, hold one's ground, keep ones possession, refusing to be moved."[1]

In the definition of 'resist', one aspect stands out to me: keep one's possession. We must know what is ours in Christ and strongly believe that the Devil isn't allowed to have it. The Devil isn't allowed to take my health because my health was purchased by the blood of Jesus and given to me as a free gift. The Devil isn't allowed to steal my joy because my joy is a fruit of the Spirit and a result of dwelling in God's presence. They are not his to take.

> "I am leaving you with a gift—peace of mind and heart. And the peace I give is a gift the world cannot give. So don't be troubled or afraid."
>
> —John 14:27 (NLT)

We live in this world, but we are not of this world, and we know full well what the world gives us.

> For everything in the world—the lust of the flesh, the lust of the eyes, and the pride of life—comes not from the Father but from the world.
>
> —1 John 2:16

Everything in this world is designed to rob us of our peace and our joy. There's always bad news on TV; there's always some crisis happening, there's always a reason to worry. If you're not careful, you'll get sucked into it and constantly battle worry and discouragement.

> "Therefore I tell you, do not worry about your life, what you will eat or drink; or about your body, what you will wear. Is not life more than food, and the body more than clothes? Look at the birds of the air; they do not sow or reap or store away in barns, and yet your heavenly Father feeds them. Are you not much more valuable than they? Can any one of you by worrying add a single hour to your life? And why do you worry about clothes? See how the flowers of the field grow. They do

> not labor or spin. Yet I tell you that not even Solomon in all his splendor was dressed like one of these. If that is how God clothes the grass of the field, which is here today and tomorrow is thrown into the fire, will he not much more clothe you—you of little faith? So do not worry, saying, 'What shall we eat?' or 'What shall we drink?' or 'What shall we wear?' For the pagans run after all these things, and your heavenly Father knows that you need them."
>
> — Matthew 6:25-32

Another change in vocabulary is needed. When the world talks about everything that can go wrong, we must remind ourselves that we live on a different plain. I am more precious to God than the birds and the flowers. I don't need to worry. I won't go without. I won't be in lack. I will always have everything I need.

If I'm a tither and a giver, I'm not part of the world's financial system. I'm part of God's financial system, and the money troubles of the world don't affect me.

Jesus purchased my healing when he took stripes on his back. The medical troubles of the world don't affect me.

If someone isn't saved, they aren't seeking God's Kingdom first, so of course, they have reason to worry. Their hope is in material things they can lose and on people who will let them down. They panic if the stock market crashes; they have no recourse against a corrupt government; they don't have the assurance of salvation; they don't have the hope and peace that transcends understanding. And, of course, it's beyond understanding because to the natural mind, it makes no sense.

They don't understand that God operates above all the things of this world. When we delight in the Lord, seek His Kingdom first, tithe, and give offerings, we are no longer in the world's economy; we're in God's economy. He will give us wisdom and discernment when it comes to decision-making. We aren't alone; we have the God of the universe on our side!

> "Anyone who listens to my teaching and follows it is wise, like a person who builds a house on solid rock. Though the rain comes in torrents and the floodwaters rise and the winds beat against that house, it won't collapse because it is built on bedrock. But anyone who hears my teaching and doesn't obey it is foolish, like a person who builds a house on sand. When the rains and floods come and the winds beat against that house, it will collapse with a mighty crash."
>
> — Matthew 7:24-27 (NLT)

Our lives are built on a firm foundation. We aren't demoralized by the cares of this world. That's why we cast our cares on the Lord. They aren't ours to bear.

---

[1] "James 4:7". Bible Hub. 2004 (https://biblehub.com/james/4-7)

Chapter Seven

Identity Crisis

There is a neurological connection with the spoken Word. When you constantly speak something, it affects the response of your body. The Devil knows how important words are; that is why it was the first thing he attacked. Are you repeating what the world says about you or what the Word says about you? Make up your mind to confess only what the Bible says.

How you speak about yourself matters. We need to identify what the Bible says about us and use that to combat any thoughts to the contrary. When you surrender your life to Christ, when you turn from sin and follow Him, there is a change that takes place. You are no longer bound to your sinful nature; you take on a new nature.

> You, however, are not in the realm of the flesh but are in the realm of the Spirit, if indeed, the Spirit of God lives in you. And if anyone does not have the Spirit of Christ, they do not belong to Christ. But if Christ is in you, then even though your

> body is subject to death because of sin, the Spirit gives life because of righteousness.
>
> — Romans 8:9-10

When you accept the gift of salvation, sin is no longer your master. You are not a sinner saved by grace; you *were* a sinner saved by grace! John opens his first letter by saying: my dear children, I write this so that you will not sin! [1 John 2:1]

Several years ago, I went through a challenging season in my life. It was an issue of mistaken identity. My flesh told me I was something, and it was a contradiction to the Word of God. I tried to find evidence that perhaps my lifelong understanding of the Bible was wrong. I wanted it to confirm what I felt rather than allow Scripture to shape how I lived.

At the time, I did not understand what it meant to declare the promises of God over my life. I did not understand how to pray. I was taught that "declaring" was a bad thing. Now I know that we can and should declare God's will and Word over our lives.

Jesus instructs us in John 16:23, "[...] Very truly I tell you, my Father will give you whatever you ask in my name." We start our prayers by approaching the Father and conclude by asking in Jesus' name. And there is power in that name.

> Therefore God exalted him to the highest place and gave him the name that is above every name, that at the name of Jesus every knee should bow, in heaven and on earth and under the earth, and every tongue acknowledge that Jesus Christ is Lord, to the glory of God the Father.
>
> — Philippians 2:9-11

In Acts 3:16, we see an account of a crippled man healed, and Peter was careful to correct him when saying that it wasn't by his hand that the man could walk again. "By faith in the name of Jesus, this man whom you see and know was made strong. It is Jesus' name and the faith that comes through him that has completely healed him, as you can all see."

I found a foundational scripture in my search for identity in the book of Colossians...

> Since, then, you have been raised with Christ, set your hearts on things above, where Christ is, seated at the right hand of God. Set your minds on things above, not on earthly things. For you died, and your life is now hidden with Christ in God."; "Put to death, therefore, whatever belongs to your earthly nature: sexual immorality, impurity, lust, evil desires and greed, which is idolatry. Because of these, the wrath of God is coming. You used to walk in these ways, in the life you once lived. But now you must also rid yourselves of all such things as these: anger, rage, malice, slander, and filthy language from your lips. Do not lie to each other, since you have taken off your old self with its practices, and have put on the new self, which is being renewed in knowledge in the image of its Creator.
>
> — Colossians 3:1-3, 5-10

Once I established that I was dealing with a sin issue, I knew I needed to overcome that sin. And something that had dragged on for years was instantly healed! I prayed these things aloud over myself because that was the truth, and anything else was a lie. Say these declarations about yourself aloud:

> I am a child of God: For ye are all the children of God by faith in Christ Jesus.
>
> — Galatians 3:26 (KJV)

I am made in His image:

> So God created man in his own image, in the image of God he created him; male and female he created them.
>
> — Genesis 1:27 (ESV)

> I am born again: Since you have been born again, not of perishable seed but of imperishable, through the living and abiding word of God.
>
> — 1 Peter 1:23 (ESV)

> I am a new creation: Therefore, if anyone is in Christ, he is a new creation. The old has passed away; behold, the new has come.
>
> — 2 Corinthians 5:17 (ESV)

> I am no longer a slave to sin: For we know that our old self was crucified with him so that the body ruled by sin might be done away with, that we should no longer be slaves to sin.
>
> — Romans 6:6

> I am free: So if the Son sets you free, you will be free indeed.
>
> —John 8:36

> I am God's masterpiece: For we are God's masterpiece. He has created us anew in Christ Jesus, so we can do the good things he planned for us long ago.
>
> — Ephesians 2:10 (NLT)

> I am redeemed: In Him, we have redemption through His blood, the forgiveness of sins, according to the riches of His grace.
>
> — Ephesians 1:7 (NKJV)

> Christ redeemed us from the curse of the law by becoming a curse for us—for it is written, "Cursed is everyone who is hanged on a tree."
>
> — Galatians 3:13 (ESV)

Things change when the revelation of who God created you to be gets in your spirit. And things change when you say it aloud over yourself and about yourself. It is almost too difficult to explain in writing, but there is strength and power that pushes behind your words when you speak them out. Because the Word of God is true, it is alive and breathing.

If you have a child, and you constantly berate them, discourage them, and tell them they are not good enough, it will shape their adult life. But if you encourage your child and remind them of what

God says about them, that they can do whatever they put their mind to, it builds their confidence and self-esteem. And when they are adults, they will remember the words spoken to them in their childhood. If that is the case, simply with words of affirmation, words inspired by the Spirit of God are much more valuable!

Chapter Eight

The Spirit of Fear

As a child, I wrestled with fear; I was afraid of everything! Especially when it was time for bed, I had trouble sleeping. My parents decided intense prayer was the only solution, so they invited a pastor to lay hands on me and pray over me. I was healed! After that, my mom had to force me out of bed every morning! But later in life, as an adult, that fear began to creep in again in the form of anxiety.

For whatever reason, fear is something that plagues and cripples many people. And we know from Scripture that it's not from God, because there are hundreds of verses that tell us not to fear. 2 Timothy 1:7 (NJKV) says, "For God has not given us a spirit of fear, but of power and of love and of a sound mind."

The Pastor prayed that verse over me. We see where fear comes from, and it's not God!

The Bible teaches us that fear is a spirit, and it is not of God. We learn in reading about the fruit of the Spirit that everything from God is the opposite of fear. Someone gripped by fear does not have joy, lacks hope, and certainly does not have peace. So we know from Scripture that living with fear is not God's will. But while living on this earth, it is ever-present oppression. That is why there are hundreds of verses instructing us not to fear.

You feel confident and emboldened when you wake up in a good mood. But what happens when your feelings tell you something different? You have to choose to believe and speak what the Bible says, even if you are not feeling it.

While writing this book, my province and nation were experiencing very challenging times. I cannot tell you how many mornings I woke up feeling good and then looked at the news or social media, and my mood quickly changed. If you are not careful, your mind goes back and forth all day.

Our instinct is to confess the negativity that we see and read. "Did you see that? Did you hear what they are planning to do? I do not know how we are going to get out of this. We're in trouble." You convince yourself of every worst-case scenario based on what you see in the natural. But God doesn't operate in the natural; He operates on a higher plane. Our faith calls down what God is doing in the supernatural, which manifests itself in the natural.

No problem or challenge that we ever face is beyond the realm of God's intervention. But God does not act based on need. If that were the case, no one on this planet would ever require anything. God acts on faith, and that faith will never return void. When we link our faith to God's power, nothing is impossible.

Therefore, we have to understand how the Bible addresses the subject of fear because our circumstances will give us plenty of opportunities to live in fear, worry, and anxiety. But we are not in covenant with the world; we are in covenant with the Lord. This is not about pumping yourself up with some rah-rah speech. Declare the Truth of God over your life, claim your promises through Christ, and speak life rather than death.

> But the fruit of the Spirit is love, joy, peace, forbearance, kindness, goodness, faithfulness, gentleness and self-control. Against such things, there is no law. Those who belong to Christ Jesus have crucified the flesh with its passions and desires. Since we live by the Spirit, let us keep in step with the Spirit.
>
> — Galatians 5:22-25

I do not see fear, worry, or anxiety in that passage. Galatians 5:16 tells us that if we walk by the Spirit, we will not gratify the desires of the flesh. Overcoming our flesh should not be seen as an impossible task. It may bark loud, but it does not have more strength than the Spirit does. The key is what you choose to submit to, and what you give into. Remember to Whom you belong. We were once under the influence of the evil one, but we are now in Christ.

> For those who are led by the Spirit of God are the children of God. The Spirit you received does not make you slaves, so that you live in fear again; rather, the Spirit you received brought about your adoption to sonship. [...]
>
> — Romans 8:14-15

We have a new Spirit because we are children of God. We can trust Him because He helps us, and freedom is guaranteed.

> Since the children have flesh and blood, he too shared in their humanity so that by his death he

> might break the power of him who holds the
> power of death—that is, the devil—and free those
> who all their lives were held in slavery by their
> fear of death.
>
> — Hebrews 2:14-15

Perhaps the biggest key is to know what is from God and what is from the Devil. If you believe something is from God when, in fact, it is an assignment from the Devil, it can mess you up. If you're under the impression that something has been given to you by God; if you believe that it's something you should have, perhaps to teach you a lesson, perhaps as a "cross to bear" or just "a part of life", why would you try to overcome it?

It is our responsibility to know what our covenant in Christ is. If our prayers do not carry any power, it is because we are not praying correctly. If you are sick and say, "God, if it's your will, please heal me," do not expect to be healed! It is our responsibility to know what God's will is, and God's Word is His will! A Christian can go their whole life without an answered prayer because they are not asking for anything. They will always get what they ask for. It is a simple truth: Jesus is the miracle worker, God is the healer, and they work as we confess the promises.[1]

> Now, this is the confidence that we have in Him, that
> if we ask anything according to His will, He
> hears us.
>
> — 1 John 5:14 (NKJV)

What should my expectation be? The most important expectation regarding God's Word is that it does not change. There are not two sets of promises, one for those who lived in Biblical times and another for the rest of us, after the Bible was completed. There is no indication anywhere in Scripture that God's power has an expiration date. Even after the rapture and during the tribulation, God still displays His might and His mercy.

> For I am the LORD, I change not. [...]
>
> — Malachi 3:6 (KJV)

> Jesus Christ is the same yesterday, today, and forever.
>
> — Hebrews 13:8 (ESV)

> He remembers his covenant forever, the promise he made, for a thousand generations.
>
> — Psalm 105:8

> That promise is not just for Israel but also for all who are children of God through faith in Jesus. "And now that you belong to Christ, you are the true children of Abraham. You are his heirs, and God's promise to Abraham belongs to you."
>
> — Galatians 3:29 (NLT)

> Whatever is good and perfect is a gift coming down to us from God our Father, who created all the lights in the heavens. He never changes or casts a shifting shadow.
>
> —James 1:17 (NLT)

> For the Lord God is a sun and shield; the LORD will

> give grace and glory; no good thing will He withhold from those who walk uprightly.
>
> — Psalm 84:11 (NKJV)

> So if you sinful people know how to give good gifts to your children, how much more will your heavenly Father give good gifts to those who ask Him.
>
> — Matthew 7:11 (NLT)

> Peace I leave with you, My peace I give to you; not as the world gives do I give to you. Let not your heart be troubled, neither let it be afraid.
>
> — John 14:27 (NKJV)

God's promises do not have an expiration date; they do not run out, and they do not run dry. Their conditions are clear: be in Christ, walk in obedience to the Lord, and submit to His ways. His hand is never too short, and His ear is not deaf to our prayers. He loves you!

---

[1] John Osteen, There's a miracle in your mouth (Houston, TX: John Osteen, 1972), 26

Chapter Nine

Does God Send Sickness?

> Praise the LORD, my soul, and forget not all his benefits—who forgives all your sins and heals all your diseases.
>
> — Psalm 103:2-3

You will never get everything you can out of life until you understand your covenant. In addition, you will never get the full treasure of the Word until you know what God gives versus what He does not.

Therefore, we need to address some of the most common misconceptions about the nature of God. The following question may be the biggest one: Does God send sickness and disease?

Until you are fully convinced that God wants you to be well, there will always be a doubt in your mind as to whether or not you will be healed. As long as there is doubt or wavering, you may never be healed.[1]

Usually perpetrated by the book of Job, Christians allow for sickness in their lives. They are more likely to use Job 1:21 (ESV) as the basis for their doctrine, "[...] Naked I came from my mother's womb, and naked shall I return. The LORD gave, and the LORD has taken away; blessed be the name of the LORD." Essentially, ignoring all the Scripture about Jesus and the Apostles healing people.

Job was not under a covenant; he was on the scene before God made His promise to Abraham. He did not have any basis in Scripture to understand what was happening to him. But the Bible is clear on who was the source of Job's trouble.

> The LORD said to Satan, "Very well, then, he is in your hands; but you must spare his life." So Satan went out from the presence of the LORD and afflicted Job with painful sores from the soles of his feet to the crown of his head.
>
> —Job 2:6-7

Satan was the thief, God was the rewarder. Job had to prove his justification through his own works. We are justified through Christ. Remember: our relationship with God changes through covenant, but God never changes!

> "And the LORD restored Job's losses when he prayed for his friends. Indeed the LORD gave Job twice as much as he had before."
>
> —Job 42:10 (NKJV)

What God allows is not the same as what He wills. And that is an important distinction. Once God made a covenant with His people, the only time He allowed sickness to touch them was a result of disobedience. But sickness itself is not from the hand of God. If it were, then He would be contradicting Himself when He said...

> "[...] for I am the LORD who heals you."
>
> — Exodus 15:26 (NKJV)

Jesus reminded us of this in Mark 3:23-24, "[...] how can Satan drive out Satan? If a kingdom is divided against itself, that kingdom cannot stand." The same being cannot be the source of both good and evil. There was no sickness in the Garden of Eden, and there will be no sickness in Heaven. So can it be a part of God's will? No, it is a result of sin and the fall of man, and the cure was provided for us when Jesus died on the cross.

> That evening they brought to him many who were oppressed by demons, and he cast out the spirits with a word and healed all who were sick. This was to fulfil what was spoken by the prophet Isaiah: "He took our illnesses and bore our diseases."
>
> — Matthew 8:16-17 (ESV)

It is a life-changing revelation when you establish that sickness is not some test of your faith or some lesson God is trying to teach you. Now I know the critics will say, "Not everyone gets healed." But not everyone is saved either; it does not mean salvation is not available for us now.

Marcy Di Michele

God's will is always to heal, though many Christians find ways to explain that away. If healing was only for Jesus to show His power, why did James give the following instruction?

> Is anyone among you sick? Let them call the elders of the church to pray over them and anoint them with oil in the name of the Lord. And the prayer offered in faith will make the sick person well; the Lord will raise them up. If they have sinned, they will be forgiven. Therefore confess your sins to each other and pray for each other so that you may be healed. The prayer of a righteous person is powerful and effective.
>
> —James 5:14-16

Sin and sickness are the twins of Satan's work, and both were defeated in the same manner at the same time.

We should also answer another common question on the subject: What about Paul's thorn in the flesh?

> [...] Therefore, in order to keep me from becoming conceited, I was given a thorn in my flesh, a messenger of Satan, to torment me. Three times I pleaded with the Lord to take it away from me. But he said to me, "My grace is sufficient for you, for my power is made perfect in weakness." Therefore I will boast all the more gladly about my weaknesses, so that Christ's power may rest on me.
>
> — 2 Corinthians 12:7-9

Paul states exactly what his thorn was; He says it was the messenger of Satan or, as translated by others, the angel of the Devil, Satan's angel, and so on. The illustration of the thorn in the flesh was a personality, the messenger of Satan. This word, used in 2 Corinthians 12:7 to describe the suffering received by Paul from this messenger of Satan, must harmonize with its same meaning in other passages. In no case does it refer to sickness or disease.[2]

The passage about Paul's thorn is used to comfort people who have prayed to be healed but have not received it. Paul asked God to remove the thorn, but God would not do it. Instead, He told Paul that His grace would be sufficient to deal with it. That leads to a dangerous doctrine that God will strengthen us to deal with sickness rather than heal us.

Therefore, even if you believe that sickness is only from Satan, an incorrect explanation of this passage will lead you to believe that God is content with you living with it and enduring it. A study of the original language will reveal that the words 'weakness' and 'infirmity', in proper context, do not refer to sickness and disease.

Paul suffered immensely for preaching the gospel. Sickness and suffering, however, are not the same thing. In Acts chapter 9, we read about Saul's miraculous conversion and the mantle placed on him.

> "But the Lord said to Ananias, "Go! This man is my chosen instrument to proclaim my name to the Gentiles and their kings and to the people of Israel. I will show him how much he must suffer for my name."
>
> — Acts 9:15-16

Paul had a specific calling, for which he suffered more intense persecution. This is not to say that we will not face any persecution; Jesus promised we would. Some Christians will face more intense persecution than others will. Some will even be martyred for their faith. But that kind of suffering implies a choice: if you choose to stand up for your faith, there is a risk of persecution. If you want to avoid any trouble, you stand down, and perhaps even practice your faith in private so that no one will notice. You have to do something for the Lord to possibly bring on the persecution!

It is a common refrain for Christians to try to explain what they are going through by comparing themselves with the extreme cases in the Bible. But they never seem to take into account the weight of Scripture. You could cite dozens of verses showing people healed, but the response will always be, what about Job? What about Paul's thorn? The Bible says nothing about Paul being sick, about him praying for healing, or about God requiring Paul to remain sick.[3]

People are so desperate to figure out why they are not healed that they search for any example to make them feel better about it. Growing up, I remember hearing Christians say that God wanted to teach us a lesson through sickness, but that is not in the Bible. God disciplines us, but never through sickness or disease.

> For the Lord disciplines the one he loves, and chastises every son whom he receives.
>
> — Hebrews 12:6 (ESV)

If we are heading for sin or refusing to submit to holiness, God chastens us. He does not randomly send sickness on a righteous, spirit-filled Christian just to test where their faith is. Our faith is not tested by that which has already been covered through the atonement. If that is how we view our loving Father, we will never have anything He wants to give us. That is why it is crucial to understand Job and Paul's situations in the proper context.

There's an assumption that since not everyone is healed, it must not be God's will to heal everyone. But not everyone gets saved either, yet we know God wills that everyone would be saved! "This is good, and it is pleasing in the sight of God our Savior, who desires all people to be saved and to come to the knowledge of the truth." – 1 Timothy 2:3-4 (ESV)

Then, one might ask, "So why don't more people get healed?" The answer: Because of the lack of teaching and preaching the truth of healing from the Bible. Let us not stand by the bed of sick people to sympathize with their pains. Let us never insinuate that it must be God's will to "take them"; or that "it will teach them patience"; or that perhaps, "they will be drawn closer to the Lord" through their sickness. Let us rather declare war on every form of sickness, and take authority over every form of demon power through the name of Jesus Christ.[4]

---

[1] T.L Osborn, Healing the Sick (Shippensburg, PA: Harrison House Publishers, 1992), 9

[2] T.L Osborn, Healing the Sick (Shippensburg, PA: Harrison House Publishers, 1992), 222

[3] T.L Osborn, Healing the Sick (Shippensburg, PA: Harrison House Publishers, 1992), 224

[4] T.L Osborn, Healing the Sick (Shippensburg, PA: Harrison House Publishers, 1992), 23

Chapter Ten

Victory over defeat

I have heard this question posed many times: Is the Christian life supposed to be hard? The question is asked because, "everyone goes through hard times." But often refer to situations that Christians don't have to endure because it's unscriptural. The Bible tells me that if I am hooked up with Jesus Christ, there are things that are not allowed to be a part of my life. But that does not mean Satan will not try.

Many people point to the fact that Paul suffered during his entire ministry and was brutally martyred. But Paul's life wasn't taken from him; he gave it up when he knew he had finished his mission.

> For I am already being poured out like a drink offering, and the time for my departure is near. I have fought the good fight, I have finished the race, I have kept the faith. Now there is in store for me the crown of righteousness, which the Lord, the righteous Judge, will award to me on that day—

> and not only to me but also to all who have longed for his appearing.
>
> — 2 Timothy 4:6-8

He could have gone to be with the Lord earlier, but he chose to stay on earth to continue his ministry to the church.

> For I know that through your prayers and God's provision of the Spirit of Jesus Christ what has happened to me will turn out for my deliverance. I eagerly expect and hope that I will in no way be ashamed, but will have sufficient courage so that now as always Christ will be exalted in my body, whether by life or by death. For to me, to live is Christ and to die is gain. If I am to go on living in the body, this will mean fruitful labor for me. Yet what shall I choose? I do not know! I am torn between the two: I desire to depart and be with Christ, which is better by far; but it is more necessary for you that I remain in the body. Convinced of this, I know that I will remain, and I will continue with all of you for your progress and joy in the faith so that through my being with you again your boasting in Christ Jesus will abound on account of me.
>
> — Philippians 1:19-26

There's a difference between a challenge and a defeat. We do face challenges in life. There are giants to slay and mountains to move. But we aren't defeated by those things. When we're in the fire, we're not burned! When we're in the lion's den, they are pillows for our heads! When we face the Red Sea, it's parted before us! We see the storm, but we command the winds and rain to be still!

Jesus told us we would face persecution as a result of following him. In addition, depending on your country, there could be a lot of persecution or very little. Jesus told us we would be hated and imprisoned because of our faith. But He also provided comfort.

> "I have told you these things, so that in me you may have peace. In this world, you will have trouble. But take heart! I have overcome the world."
>
> —John 16:33

The Bible also says we should consider it joy when we face persecution, (James 1:2) so how can we declare it a hard life? Those who persevere are considered blessed. We rejoice when our faith is tested through persecution.

We don't deny the existence of sickness, poverty, or lack. We simply place the Word of God against those things and say what God said. What are you saying about your situation? There is a law at work, and you must be careful because you'll create what you're speaking about. I'm not saying to lie regarding what may be happening to you. I'm saying to read God's Word and agree with God.

Your words must line up with God's Word. If all you speak is negativity, it will be challenging to flip the switch and activate your faith. You'll be defeated before you even get in the fight.

Joel 3:10 (NKJV) states, "[...] Let the weak say, 'I am strong.'" That verse doesn't say, "Let the weak say I'm not weak," it says they should say, "I am strong!" You have to learn to use your mouth and agree with God. How many times did God say to not fear but to be strong and courageous? You may feel weak in the natural, you may be up against a challenge, but if God says you are strong, you have to say: I am strong!

The doctor says you're sick, but the Bible says that by His stripes you are healed. You aren't denying the doctor's report; you're simply agreeing with God, reminding yourself of what God says about that challenge. You send God's Word out of your mouth, and it will produce. Jesus won the victory over Satan the day the veil was torn in two; remember who has the victory.

> [...] That power is the same as the mighty strength he exerted when he raised Christ from the dead and seated him at his right hand in the heavenly realms, far above all rule and authority, power and dominion, and every name that is invoked, not only in the present age but also in the one to come. And God placed all things under his feet and appointed him to be head over everything for the church, which is his body, the fullness of him who fills everything in every way.
>
> — Ephesians 1:19-23

The same authority Jesus had, we have as his body. He even said this to his disciples before His death and resurrection.

> "I have given you authority to trample on snakes and scorpions and to overcome all the power of the enemy; nothing will harm you."
>
> — Luke 10:19

Do you understand your authority? So many Christians don't realize what they carry inside of them through salvation in Christ Jesus. If you view the Devil as some powerful enemy that "can't possibly be overcome," your life will reflect that. Anything that happens to you will defeat you. There has to be a moment where you take your place as a child of God and a servant of the Lord Jesus Christ.

The Devil realizes he cannot hold in bondage a believer who knows their authority in Christ Jesus. Such a believer is aware that they are seated with Christ in heavenly places and the Devil is a defeated foe under their feet. Furthermore, this believer is convinced that no work of the enemy can prevail against them carrying out God's will on the earth.[1]

The Devil is not on equal footing with God; he's a created being, and more than that, he is a defeated foe. There's no wrestling match between Jesus and the Devil; it's not a fair fight. The moment that veil was torn in two, the Devil lost his authority. But now, he works through deception, and part of that deception is convincing Christians that they have no recourse against his schemes.

We're not moved by how we feel. The Bible says in 2 Corinthians that we walk by faith, not by sight. God's Word and God's promises do not change depending on your circumstances. The Word of God is always anointed, so you don't have to worry about how you feel. Once you start speaking the Word out loud, the anointing will be there.

Mountains are immovable objects in the natural. When Jesus instructed his disciples to speak to the mountain, He was letting them know that you don't speak what you see; you speak what Scripture says. You can change situations by your speaking. God gave man the ability to speak words; animals can't, plants can't, fish can't, monkeys can't. It's something exclusive to human beings.

If you take the posture of a victim, you'll live a victim's life. But if you take the posture of a victor and a champion, you'll live a victorious life. You won't be easily beaten down. The way you view yourself will determine how you respond to life.

If your car breaks down, someone with a victim mentality will say stuff like, "This always happens to me; nothing ever goes right!" But someone with a victor's mentality will never allow an inconvenience to derail their life or destroy their confession. Victims expect things to go wrong, whether they realize it or not, because they've already decided they're at a disadvantage. A victor expects that everything will work out.

Many times, we use victimhood as a crutch. Maybe for an excuse as to why we haven't succeeded or accomplished the goals we had set for ourselves. Maybe we crave pity and sympathy. Sometimes it's easier to just stay as we are rather than make a change. That was my problem for years. I didn't think it was possible to overcome the issues I was facing, and I just grew accustomed to wallowing. When I confided in people, I didn't want a solution; I just wanted them to feel bad for me. But that's not the posture a child of God should ever take.

Think about the story of Joseph, for example. He had every reason to see himself as a victim; He had every reason to give up. He knew God gave him a dream, but it seemed like everything that happened in his life moved him further away from the fruition of that dream.

His brothers betrayed him and sold him as a slave. They pretended he was dead. I think any of us would feel alone and worthless. He had every right to see himself as a victim. Despite being sold as a slave, he quickly rose to prominence as the head of Potiphar's estate. But that glory was short-lived; Potiphar's wife took a liking to Joseph and tried to seduce him. Being a righteous man, Joseph refused, so out of humiliation, Potiphar's wife accused Joseph of raping her, and he was thrown into prison! Could you imagine Joseph's reaction? Things were finally looking up, and he ended up worse off than before. The worst part was that he had done nothing wrong!

Joseph found favor while in prison but was forgotten about and stayed there much longer than he should have. He eventually rose to a high position within the prison and saw the fulfillment of his dreams. There's no record of Joseph complaining or speaking negatively. He confessed the exact opposite with one of the most commonly quoted verses in the Bible:

> As for you, you meant evil against me, but God meant it for good, to bring it about that many people should be kept alive, as they are today.
>
> — Genesis 50:20 (ESV)

That's a powerful reminder of how to respond to challenges. Joseph spoke a positive confession. But so often, our first response is to complain about the situation. God does not respond to complaints.

> Do everything without complaining and arguing.
>
> — Philippians 2:14 (NLT)

It is human instinct to complain. But what does it ever accomplish? We may think it will make us feel better, but it usually leaves us feeling worse. Joseph's predicament reminds me of a truth found in Psalms...

> Blessed is the one who does not walk in step with the wicked or stand in the way that sinners take or sit in the company of mockers, but whose delight is in the law of the LORD, and who meditates on his law day and night. That person is like a tree

> planted by streams of water, which yields its fruit
> in season and whose leaf does not wither—whatever they do prospers.
>
> — Psalms 1:1-3

Joseph had no dry seasons, no matter where he was; he found favor, was promoted, and delivered. And like many characters in the Old Testament, he was under the old covenant; before the Messiah had arrived and the Holy Spirit descended. How much more so should we expect Joseph's favor and then some?

> Surely, LORD, you bless the righteous; you surround
> them with your favor as with a shield.
>
> — Psalm 5:12

We have to change our vocabulary: I am blessed! I won't have any dry seasons! God's favor surrounds me like a shield! I will always bear fruit!

---

[1] Kenneth E. Hagin, The Believers Authority (Tulsa, OK: Faith Library Publications, 1986), 58

Chapter Eleven

I Can Do All Things

Another Scripture often debated over context is found in Philippians...

> I can do all things through Christ who strengthens me.
>
> — Philippians 4:13 (NKJV)

There are varied interpretations of this verse. One recent commentary stated that it should be applied to encourage Christians who face failure or have had their dreams crushed. It spoke of the danger in teaching Christians that anything is possible because they'll inevitably end up disappointed when things don't work out the way they'd envisioned. In other words, limit your expectations, and don't assume you'll get what you want out of life.

Paul wrote the book of Philippians while he was in prison. Paul was writing with a sense of joy, despite the persecution he faced. He encouraged the believers to rejoice. He also wanted to honor the church of Philippi for their financial support. He didn't shy away from acknowledging his hardship, but he never complained, either. He rejoiced in his suffering because everything he did was for the Lord.

Paul expressed the reality of God's strength helping him get through the persecution he faced. But it didn't end there. He wanted the believers to know that Christianity was divine, living, dynamic, and liberating; it was not a dead, dry human religion of rituals. Someone without the power to deliver men from sin, sickness, poverty, and want, is not of God.[1]

The temptation to interpret the book of Philippians is to focus on Paul's tribulations and his finding contentment, even in lack. But he was never in need. He worked to support himself and had help from the church offerings. The focus of the book is on rejoicing. When Paul spoke of persecutions he endured in 2 Timothy 11, he said. "The Lord rescued [him] from them all." God gives us the strength to overcome all opposition. God's power isn't limited to rescue. He's the God of the impossible!

> Very truly I tell you, whoever believes in me will do the works I have been doing, and they will do even greater things than these because I am going to the Father. And I will do whatever you ask in my name, so that the Father may be glorified in the Son. You may ask me for anything in my name, and I will do it.
>
> —John 14:12-14

When we operate according to the will of God, and ask without doubting, we can have what we say. You have to align yourself with the Word of God and the will of God. If you ask God for the ability to fly when you jump off a mountain, you won't live to tell the story because it is not in alignment with God's Word. That's why Jesus reminded Satan that we must not put God to the test.

God wants you to live holy; He wants you to live the right way. God also wants to bless you; He wants to prosper you. It's not one or the other. There's a mistaken belief that we should only seek God's face, not His hand. But you don't have to choose. As a result of seeking His face, you will receive blessings. It's a package deal.

> That he would grant you, according to the riches of his glory, to be strengthened with might by his Spirit in the inner man.
>
> — Ephesians 3:16 (KJV)

> Being strengthened with all power according to his glorious might so that you may have great endurance and patience.
>
> — Colossians 1:11

> I thank Christ Jesus our Lord, who has strengthened me, because He considered me faithful, putting me into service.
>
> — 1 Timothy 1:12 (NASB)

> My flesh and my heart may fail, but God is the strength of my heart and my portion forever.
>
> — Psalm 73:26

We're all guilty of taking a verse out of context to prove a point. In addition to the study of Hermeneutics discussed earlier, it's also helpful to seek out the original language. After all, the Bible wasn't written in English!

The word "strength," in the original language, translates to: "Fill with power, strengthen, make strong." The word used is dynamóō, which means: "sharing power; to impart ability (make able); empowered." The phrase "all things" translates to: "all, the whole, every kind of." The word used there is pás, which means: "every part of a totality. The emphasis of the total picture."[2]

When Paul spoke these words, he was in prison. He had experienced much persecution for the gospel. He went through times when he had plenty and others when he had little. In prior verses, he was lamenting over the church that wasn't giving him enough money. Paul understood that his specific ministry was going to be difficult.

> "I will show him how much he must suffer for my name."
>
> — Acts 9:16

Philippians 4:13 is an encouragement; we are equipped to be overcomers. We don't ignore the reality of Paul's situation. It doesn't mean that God strengthens you to do whatever you feel like and is bound to support it. All must be done according to the will of God.

It would contradict the rest of Scripture for Paul to write from a place of defeat. He wasn't saying, "When things don't work out, don't worry, God will be there for you." If we are more than conquerors through Christ, we can't be defeated by the Devil.

Paul was reminding the Philippians of the sufficiency of Christ, that we don't need anything else but Him, understanding the fullness and power that comes through Him. People filled with the spirit of religion will use that as an affirmation to have contentment when they're poor, sick, or in constant turmoil, thinking it's God's plan for their lives.

Context is not relative. It's not based on how you feel or on your experiences. If you want to know the truth, you have to read the entirety of the Word of God and allow Spirit to come alive inside of you. Pray and believe for faith and understanding.

Jesus came so we can have life (both present physical, and future spiritual life, exert a saving power spoken of earthly life), and have it to the fullest: More, greater, excessive, abundant, exceedingly, preeminent, advantage!

Why do we cling to the sufferings and disdain the blessings? It's because of the defeated and powerless mindset perpetuated by the spirit of religion, which is the very thing Jesus came to destroy.

Everyone likes to quote the words of Jesus, whether to prove a point or to catch someone in a contradiction. They also cite the words He didn't say to formulate a personal ideology as if Jesus had a completely different belief system from God the Father. But proper Bible application is to view everything in light of the *entire* Word of God.

The typical arguments regarding the commands of Jesus are one or all of the following: "Jesus only meant that for His disciples; Jesus only meant that for the Jewish people; Jesus didn't mention that specifically, so God must have changed His mind about it."

Jesus' teachings throughout the gospels are directed toward three groups of people:

1. His disciples;
2. The multitudes of Jewish people;
3. The Pharisees and Sadducees.

So how could we know if any of those commands are meant for Christians today?

> Then the eleven disciples went to Galilee, to the mountain where Jesus had told them to go. Then Jesus came to them and said, "[...] go and make disciples of all nations, baptizing them in the name of the Father and of the Son and of the Holy Spirit, and teaching them to obey everything I have commanded you. [...]"
>
> — Matthew 28:16, 18-20

The Great Commission is still carried out, even though it was a command given directly to the disciples and no one else. But any confusion is cleared up by Jesus' words in John 8:31 (NLT): Jesus said to the people who believed in him, "You are truly my disciples if you remain faithful to my teachings."

What about us as Gentiles? Should we also hold to the teachings given to the Jewish people? Jesus had many interactions with Gentiles throughout His ministry, and they all experienced the same blessings as the Jews. Paul addressed this in the book of Romans:

> After all, is God the God of the Jews only? Isn't he also the God of the Gentiles? Of course, he is.
>
> — Romans 3:29 (NLT)

> For there is no difference between Jew and Gentile— the same Lord is Lord of all and richly blesses all who call on him.
>
> — Romans 10:12

Peter also covered it with his teaching in Acts 10:34-35: Then Peter began to speak: "I now realize how true it is that God does not show favoritism but accepts from every nation the one who fears him and does what is right."

And lastly, what about Jesus' words directed to the religious people who wanted to kill Him? Those must be weighed in light of the entirety of Scripture, and every response He gave. Whether about marriage, the law, or love and compassion, it is in keeping with the principles laid out by God throughout His Word.

> Very truly I tell you, whoever believes in me will do the works I have been doing, and they will do even greater things than these because I am going to the Father. And I will do whatever you ask in my name, so that the Father may be glorified in the Son. You may ask me for anything in my name, and I will do it.
>
> —John 14:12-14

When Jesus sent out the seventy-two in Luke 10, He made an important point in verse 2: He told them, "The harvest is plentiful, but the workers are few. Ask the Lord of the harvest, therefore, to send out workers into his harvest field."

Jesus' commands were not exclusive to the twelve disciples or the seventy-two others. But at that time, they were the ones who had left everything to follow Him; therefore, they were the ones He was sending out. To believe that it no longer counts for us today makes no sense! Why would He tell them to pray for more workers? He knew we would be carrying out the work now!

The promise that God gave in Psalm 91:13, "You will tread on the lion and the cobra; you will trample the great lion and the serpent," was confirmed by Jesus in Luke 10:19 (ESV), "Behold, I have given you authority to tread on serpents and scorpions, and over all the power of the enemy, and nothing shall hurt you."

He gave us authority over all the power of the enemy. The work started by the disciples and continued by the early believers is still moving today. To believe anything less would strip God of His power.

---

[1] Finis Jennings Dake, Dake's Annotated Reference Bible (Lawrenceville, GA: Dake Publishing Inc, 2014), 381

[2] "Philippians 4:13". Bible Hub. 2004. (https://biblehub.com/philippians/4-13)

Chapter Twelve

A Good Father

> Then Peter began to speak: "I now realize how true it is that God does not show favoritism."
>
> — Acts 10:34

God doesn't put our names in a hat and then pick one every day to see whom He will bless. Everyone has access to the same blessings and the same favor, but there are ways to unlock the favor that comes from the Lord.

> "Because he loves me," says the LORD, "I will rescue him; I will protect him, for he acknowledges my name. He will call on me, and I will answer him; I will be with him in trouble, I will deliver him and honor him. With long life, I will satisfy him and show him my salvation."
>
> — Psalm 91:14-16

> "You may ask me for anything in my name, and I will do it. If you love me, keep my commands. And I will ask the Father, and he will give you another advocate to help you and be with you forever—the Spirit of truth. [...]"
>
> — John 14:14-17

Blessing is attached to obeying God; it's a natural outpouring of loving God. When you sincerely love God, there is a desire to please Him.

> Jesus replied, "Anyone who loves me will obey my teaching. My Father will love them, and we will come to them and make our home with them."
>
> — John 14:23

> [...] We have confidence before God and receive from him anything we ask because we keep his commands and do what pleases him.
>
> — 1 John 3:21-22

> He replied, "Blessed rather are those who hear the word of God and obey it."
>
> — Luke 11:28

> Praise the LORD! Blessed is the man who fears the LORD, who greatly delights in his commandments!
>
> — Psalm 112:1 (ESV)

> Keep this Book of the Law always on your lips; meditate on it day and night, so that you may be careful to do everything written in it. Then you will be prosperous and successful.
>
> — Joshua 1:8

> But from everlasting to everlasting the LORD's love is with those who fear him, and his righteousness with their children's children—with those who keep his covenant and remember to obey his precepts.
>
> — Psalm 103:17-18

> But without faith, it is impossible to please Him, for he who comes to God must believe that He is, and that He is a rewarder of those who diligently seek Him.
>
> — Hebrews 11:6 (NKJV)

First, we must come to God and seek after Him. He isn't a genie obligated to grant our wish. He desires to be in a relationship with us. We are on this earth to give glory to God. He blesses us because He loves us. Second, we must believe God is who He said He is. Once you understand that God is a good God, that He is a rewarder, and He wants to bless you, you have to make sure your prayers aren't undone by your words. You can spend hours in prayer, reading Scriptures out loud, and speaking God's promises, but it will be undone if your words don't back what you pray.

> But when you ask, you must believe and not doubt, because the one who doubts is like a wave of the

> sea, blown and tossed by the wind. That person should not expect to receive anything from the Lord. Such a person is double-minded and unstable in all they do.
>
> —James 1:6-8

I knew someone who used to pray incredible prayers filled with Scripture and declarations. But afterward, he said, "I hope it works out; we'll see what happens." He just undid everything he prayed. He didn't believe what he was reciting. His prayers had a powerful tone, but his heart was full of doubt.

There's an old saying, "You can't stop the birds from flying over your head, but you can keep them from making a nest in your hair."... Doubt is not hard to come by, all you have to do is look at your natural circumstances, and doubt can seep in easily. Peter was all gung-ho to walk on water until he looked around and saw the wind and the waves.

> "Lord, if it's you," Peter replied, "tell me to come to you on the water." "Come," he said. Then Peter got down out of the boat, walked on the water and came toward Jesus. But when he saw the wind, he was afraid and, beginning to sink, cried out, "Lord, save me!" Immediately Jesus reached out his hand and caught him. "You of little faith," he said, "why did you doubt?"
>
> — Matthew 14:28-31

The key is ensuring doubt never comes out of your mouth. That's why it's crucial to know what the Word of God says, what God's nature is, and His will and promises.

> Before you ask God for anything, build a case from the Word of God. Do you have sufficient Scripture to back up what you are praying for? If not, then you have no business praying for it! But if you do, then you have no business doubting God's integrity to answer.
>
> — Evangelist TJ Malcangi

I used to live in a basement apartment. My landlords would often make a lot of noise, which prompted me to yell and bang on the ceiling. That's how we should treat wrong thoughts that creep into our minds. Tell them to shut up!

There's no need to wonder if you should stay sick, broke, or depressed. There's no need to wonder whether we should live with it or endure it. There's a difference between persecution and suffering from something that Jesus already triumphed over on the cross. If Jesus died to it, why are you living with it?

Chapter Thirteen

The Promised Land

I used to love posting Christian quotes on social media. I didn't realize the majority of them aren't Biblical. Many quotes try to explain the difficulties we face as Christians. They're often based on emotion or in reaction to an experience.

Here's one I used to like: "You can't see the promised land without the wilderness." But do we understand why the Israelites had to wander in the desert for forty years? The journey should have only taken them eleven days!

> "Not one of those who saw my glory and the signs I performed in Egypt and in the wilderness but who disobeyed me and tested me ten times—not one of them will ever see the land I promised on oath to their ancestors. No one who has treated me with contempt will ever see it."
>
> — Numbers 14:22-23

God hadn't sent the Holy Spirit yet; Jesus hadn't been sacrificed once and for all, yet. The Israelites disobeyed God; they built idols, doubted God's power, and lacked faith. God purposely led them a long way to start the journey. Why? Because He knew they didn't believe that He would deliver them.

> When Pharaoh let the people go, God did not lead them on the road through the Philistine country, though that was shorter. For God said, "If they face war, they might change their minds and return to Egypt."
>
> — Exodus 13:17

We'll never know what would have happened if the Israelites had trusted God and obeyed Him.

Once you receive salvation through faith in Jesus, you enter into covenant with God. You are no longer in bondage to the curse of the law. You've been set free from sin, sickness, and suffering. Your faith isn't tested by that which has already been covered in the atonement. The Bible teaches persecution must be considered as joy. Jesus said to rejoice and be glad. Paul said to rejoice. But getting your butt kicked by the Devil in an area he's not allowed to touch you is not joyful.

When you become a child of God, you change your address; you don't live in the valley anymore. You might be passing through, but you can't stay there; it's not where you belong. God wants to set you on the mountaintop. He wants to take you from glory to glory, strength to strength, and everlasting to everlasting.

> Oh, put God to the test and see how kind he is! See for yourself the way his mercies shower down on all who trust in him. If you belong to the Lord,

> reverence him; for everyone who does this has everything he needs. Even strong young lions sometimes go hungry, but those of us who reverence the Lord will never lack any good thing.
>
> — Psalm 34:8-10 (TLB)

Psalm 23 says, "[...] though I walk through the darkest valley [...]." Paul praised his way out of shackles and prison! Daniel was unharmed in the lion's den for a whole night! —He probably used a lion as a pillow. The day Shadrach, Meshach, and Abednego were put into the fiery furnace, they came out of it alive, they didn't smell of smoke, and not even one hair on their heads had burned!

Never forget: because of the power of God through His Spirit in us, we have dominion over the attack of the enemy.

> I have given you authority to trample on snakes and scorpions and to overcome all the power of the enemy; nothing will harm you.
>
> — Luke 10:19

We have no problem accepting the things the Devil uses to destroy us. We own sickness, depression, anxiety, fear, and discouragement. But when God has good gifts for us, we say, "No, I don't believe in that. God doesn't want to prosper us; that's heresy. God doesn't want to heal us; that's not for today." We're even reluctant to embrace the gift of the Holy Spirit.

> So if you sinful people know how to give good gifts to your children, how much more will your heavenly Father give good gifts to those who ask him.
>
> — Matthew 7:11 (NLT)

Marcy Di Michele

When the Spirit moves, we immediately assume it can't be of God. But when the Devil buries us with trials, we wrap our arms around them. Why believe God sends struggles to teach us a lesson? Believe He wants to deliver us from the grip of the enemy!

> But the Lord is faithful; he will strengthen you and guard you from the evil one.
>
> — 2 Thessalonians 3:3 (NLT)

Why? Because our faith is easily shaken; we see too much pain and struggle around us and not enough miracles. We don't see miracles because we don't have the faith to believe it's possible. We operate with a weak, watered-down version of faith, so much so that when anyone rises with an increased level of faith to claim God's promises, we label them a false teacher.

Never forget: Our circumstances will not change the promises of God.

When Peter stepped out onto the water, he stepped out with a heart full of faith. But as soon as he began to look around and saw the wind and the waves, his faith crumbled.

> [...] Then Peter got down out of the boat, walked on the water and came toward Jesus. But when he saw the wind, he was afraid and, beginning to sink, cried out, "Lord, save me!" Immediately Jesus reached out his hand and caught him. "You of little faith," he said, "why did you doubt?"
>
> — Matthew 14:29-31

The Bible teaches that doubt is like being double-minded, which in the Greek translation means to "waver, to be uncertain or half-hearted."[1]

> But let him ask in faith, with no doubting, for the one who doubts is like a wave of the sea that is driven and tossed by the wind. For that person must not suppose that he will receive anything from the Lord; he is a double-minded man, unstable in all his ways.
>
> — James 1:6-8 (ESV)

Faith always looks beyond the natural because it operates in the supernatural. Our minds can never comprehend it. If we try to define faith with our human minds, we'll never figure it out. If we try to use intellect to explain the spiritual, we'll end up pushing the Spirit out because it doesn't make earthly sense.

What happened when the disciples were in a boat facing the storm? Did Jesus tell them, "This is good for you; it's going to help build your faith. You can't have a testimony without a test." No! He rebuked the storm and commanded it to be still.

> He replied, "You of little faith, why are you so afraid?" Then he got up and rebuked the winds and the waves, and it was completely calm.
>
> — Matthew 8:26

One of the most misunderstood verses in the Bible is Exodus 14:14.

Marcy Di Michele

> The LORD will fight for you; you need only to be still.
>
> — Exodus 14:14

But keep reading.

> Then the LORD said to Moses, "Why are you crying out to me? Tell the Israelites to move on. Raise your staff and stretch out your hand over the sea to divide the water so that the Israelites can go through the sea on dry ground."
>
> — Exodus 14:15-16

We need to shed this mindset of hanging out in the desert and thinking that it's God's will for us to be there. We need to get moving, activate our faith, and believe God will deliver us. Beyond that, we need to understand our inheritance as a child of God, that the Devil can't touch us unless we allow him to.

> If you say, "The LORD is my refuge," and you make the Most High your dwelling, no harm will overtake you, no disaster will come near your tent.
>
> — Psalm 91:9-10

Being a Christian doesn't guarantee a perfect life; there's an enemy of our souls looking to take us down; there's a promise of persecution. But that overcoming persecution produces perseverance, character and hope. Just as Peter said in his first letter: These have come so that the proven genuineness of your faith, of greater worth than gold, which perishes even though refined by fire, may result in praise, glory and honor when Jesus Christ is revealed [1 Peter 1:7]. We come out stronger!

> For every child of God defeats this evil world, and we achieve this victory through our faith.
>
> — 1 John 5:4 (NLT)

Though I have not faced a fraction of what our brothers and sisters in other countries have endured, at the time of writing this book, I received a hefty fine and day in court for going to church. That was a test of faith! Do I believe God is going to take care of me? Do I stand on the conviction of His Word? Will I bow to the threats of wicked governments? I know I am victorious through Christ Jesus and the power of the Holy Spirit, and strong in his might. I will not bow to Baal or kiss his feet!

———————

[1] "James 1:6". Bible Hub. 2004 (https://biblehub.com/james/1-6)

Chapter Fourteen

Overcoming Giants

Remember, faith doesn't deny circumstances. Faith doesn't pretend we don't feel anything. But we cannot allow ourselves to be dictated by circumstances or guided by feelings. There are giants in everyone's promised land, but we can use our faith to drive them out.

When David faced Goliath, he didn't deny the giant's existence. David acknowledged there was a giant, but in a defiant way rather than a defeated one, as all the other men spoke of Goliath.

> David asked the men standing near him, "What will be done for the man who kills this Philistine and removes this disgrace from Israel? Who is this uncircumcised Philistine that he should defy the armies of the living God?"
>
> — 1 Samuel 17:26

David then spoke confidently, knowing God would help him, just as He had in the past. He knew what he was up against, yet he was full of encouragement.

> David said to Saul, "Let no one lose heart on account of this Philistine; your servant will go and fight him."
>
> — 1 Samuel 17:32

David never mentioned his shortcomings, and he didn't glorify the enemy. How many times do we magnify bad news? That's a surefire way to limit your faith. If all you speak about is how bad or difficult or terrible something is, why would you suddenly be able to flip the switch and speak faith towards it?

> "Your servant has killed both the lion and the bear; this uncircumcised Philistine will be like one of them, because he has defied the armies of the living God. The LORD who rescued me from the paw of the lion and the paw of the bear will rescue me from the hand of this Philistine." [...]
>
> — 1 Samuel 17:36-37

Saul tried to discourage him, yet David was undeterred. Be careful who you allow into your inner circle; many people are discouraging by nature. Most are unaware, while some are intentional. They'll always be there to point out why something will be too hard, why you aren't qualified, or what could go wrong.

David's confidence was not in his ability or strength. Rather, he understood Who was on his side. He understood just how much stronger and more powerful God was than any enemy he could come up against.

> David said to the Philistine, "You come against me with sword and spear and javelin, but I come against you in the name of the LORD Almighty, the God of the armies of Israel, whom you have defied. This day the LORD will deliver you into my hands, and I'll strike you down and cut off your head. This very day I will give the carcasses of the Philistine army to the birds and the wild animals, and the whole world will know that there is a God in Israel. All those gathered here will know that it is not by sword or spear that the LORD saves; for the battle is the LORD's, and he will give all of you into our hands."
>
> — 1 Samuel 17:45-47

What an amazing statement! David believed in his heart that God would deliver him, and he spoke it out of his mouth. Are you more focused on the giant, or on the God who will deliver you from the giant? Do you speak more about what the Devil is doing or about what Jesus has already done? Many seemingly insurmountable giants can get in our way. It's easy to fix our thoughts on how tough the giant is.

> So we say with confidence, "The Lord is my helper; I will not be afraid. What can mere mortals do to me?"
>
> — Hebrews 13:6

> Surely the righteous will never be shaken; they will be remembered forever. They will have no fear of bad news; their hearts are steadfast, trusting in the LORD. Their hearts are secure, they will have no fear; in the end they will look in triumph on their foes.
>
> — Psalm 112:6-8

> I sought the LORD, and he answered me; he delivered me from all my fears. Those who look to him are radiant; their faces are never covered with shame.
>
> — Psalm 34:4-5

> The LORD is my light and my salvation; whom shall I fear? The LORD is the stronghold of my life; of whom shall I be afraid?
>
> — Psalm 27:1 (ESV)

> For I, the LORD your God, hold your right hand; it is I who say to you, "Fear not, I am the one who helps you."
>
> — Isaiah 41:13 (ESV)

> But now in Christ Jesus you who once were far away have been brought near by the blood of Christ.
>
> — Ephesians 2:13

People are desperate to identify with anything because it gives them a sense of worth. That's why they support trendy causes or identify themselves by their race or sexual orientation. They don't know their true identity lies in their redemption through Christ, so they seek it elsewhere. How you identify yourself is going to shape your life. Is your identity rooted in what God says about you, or is it rooted in your job, income, family, reputation, or circumstances?

The Devil's end game is separation; God's end game is restoration. We were separated from God, but we have been reconciled to Him, and we now have a new identity. Speak that identity.

> I am a royal priesthood: But you are a chosen generation, a royal priesthood, a holy nation, His own special people, that you may proclaim the praises of Him who called you out of darkness into His marvelous light.
>
> — 1 Peter 2:9 (NKJV)

> I have the mind of Christ: For, "Who has known the mind of the Lord so as to instruct him?" But we have the mind of Christ.
>
> — 1 Corinthians 2:16

Claiming your new identity will cause a change in your vocabulary. Jesus never said, "I don't know what to do; how are we going to handle this; we're in big trouble." If we have the mind of Christ, we shouldn't speak like that either. Rather, because we are filled with the Spirit and live in submission to God, we shouldn't find ourselves in situations where we don't know what we need to do. Not only will we receive the necessary wisdom, but we'll know from God's Word how we should respond.

> If any of you lacks wisdom, you should ask God, who gives generously to all without finding fault, and it will be given to you.
>
> —James 1:5

> I am a friend of God: "I no longer call you servants, because a servant does not know his master's business. Instead, I have called you friends, for everything that I learned from my Father I have made known to you. You did not choose me, but I chose you and appointed you so that you might go and bear fruit—fruit that will last—and so that whatever you ask in my name the Father will give you."
>
> —John 15:15-16

Ephesians Chapter 1 provides a great outline of who we are in Christ. Have you ever been rejected in your life, maybe by friends, parents, or employers? According to Scripture, "he chose us in him before the creation of the world." Rejection may have been a part of your former life, but your new life in Christ says that "you were marked in him with a seal."

Verse 23 reminds us that we are the body of Christ, "the fullness of him." It makes it more difficult to put yourself down now, doesn't it? It's an insult to the sacrifice of Christ for us to degrade or demean ourselves.

Have you ever thought you were a loser, worthless, or useless? I sure have, but I needed to learn that my identity rests in the finished work of Christ on the cross. I'm not a worm, or dirt, or not good enough. I used to be all those things before coming to Christ. I was unworthy and undeserving. But not anymore, I'm a new creation, and that's a crucial distinction. There's no anointing on self-deprecation. It doesn't make you sound more humble; you're going against the Bible.

Ephesians chapter 2 lets us know that there's a doing away with our sinful life and newness in Christ, thanks to His wonderful grace.

> All of us also lived among them at one time, gratifying the cravings of our flesh and following its desires and thoughts. Like the rest, we were by nature deserving of wrath. But because of his great love for us, God, who is rich in mercy, made us alive with Christ even when we were dead in transgressions—it is by grace you have been saved.
>
> — Ephesians 2:3-5

Can you ever justify calling yourself a worm after reading verse 6?: "And God raised us up with Christ and seated us with him in the heavenly realms in Christ Jesus." How many worms are seated in heavenly places? It's nothing that we've done on our own; not by our own merit or by our own strength, which we see in verses 8-9: "For it is by grace you have been saved, through faith—and this is not from yourselves, it is the gift of God—not by works, so that no one can boast."

> Consequently, you are no longer foreigners and strangers, but fellow citizens with God's people and also members of his household, built on the foundation of the apostles and prophets, with Christ Jesus himself as the chief cornerstone. In him the whole building is joined together and rises to become a holy temple in the Lord. And

> in him you too are being built together to become a dwelling in which God lives by his Spirit.
>
> — Ephesians 2:19-22

Isn't that amazing? We are citizens of Heaven, a holy temple. Maybe you still wonder what right we have to approach God with our requests. Ephesians Chapter 3 easily clears that up in verse 12: "In him and through faith in him we may approach God with freedom and confidence." Remember that part of Jesus' work was to reconcile us back to the Father. He bridged the gap that no rule or regulation could bridge.

I sincerely believe that the main reason our prayers aren't answered is that we incorrectly approach the throne of God. We don't understand the power that is available to us. As a result, we pray weak, ineffectual prayers and live in a constant state of struggle and sadness.

Ephesians 3:16-21 clears up any confusion:

> I pray that out of his glorious riches he may strengthen you with power through his Spirit in your inner being, so that Christ may dwell in your hearts through faith. And I pray that you, being rooted and established in love, may have power, together with all the Lord's holy people, to grasp how wide and long and high and deep is the love of Christ, and to know this love that surpasses knowledge—that you may be filled to the measure of all the fullness of God. Now to him who is able to do immeasurably more than all we ask or imagine, according to his power that is at work within us, to him be glory in the church and

> in Christ Jesus throughout all generations, forever
> and ever! Amen.
>
> — Ephesians 3:16-21

More than we could ask or imagine! That's not wishful thinking, nor is it a selfish notion. It is the outflow of life in Christ. Have you ever heard anyone say that they are under a generational curse? They speak about the curse but rarely about breaking it.

> For though we walk in the flesh, we do not war
> according to the flesh. For the weapons of our
> warfare are not carnal but mighty in God for
> pulling down strongholds, casting down arguments
> and every high thing that exalts itself
> against the knowledge of God, bringing every
> thought into captivity to the obedience of Christ.
>
> — 2 Corinthians 10:3-5 (NKJV)

Demonic strongholds have no place in the life of a child of God. Once you are saved, you have been blessed, and the Bible says that we cannot curse that which God has blessed.

> I have received a command to bless; he has blessed,
> and I cannot change it.
>
> — Numbers 23:20

> Praise be to the God and Father of our Lord Jesus
> Christ, who has blessed us in the heavenly realms
> with every spiritual blessing in Christ.
>
> — Ephesians 1:3

Marcy Di Michele

Say: I am blessed!

> So that in Christ Jesus the blessing of Abraham might come to the Gentiles so that we might receive the promised Spirit through faith.
>
> — Galatians 3:14 (ESV)

The moment you choose to be saved, your address changes. Your name is now registered in Heaven. You're not who you used to be. You are no longer subject to what you used to be subjected to.

> "Behold, I have given you authority to tread on serpents and scorpions, and over all the power of the enemy, and nothing shall hurt you. Nevertheless, do not rejoice in this, that the spirits are subject to you, but rejoice that your names are written in heaven".
>
> — Luke 10:19-20 (ESV)

Chapter Fifteen

The Blessing of God

The Devil works through deception. I spent many years being deceived, particularly regarding sickness and prosperity. The Devil uses people and establishes systems to deceive us.

The government wants you sick and broke, so you'll depend on handouts for money and depend on pharmaceuticals for health. God wants you healthy and prosperous, so you'll be dependent on Him for the provision and depend on the blood of Jesus for healing. No wonder the Devil uses other Christians to call "health and wealth" a false doctrine; he wants us to view man as our source instead of trusting in God alone. If your faith is weak in any area, you won't have dominion over that area.

If the church is weak in understanding health and finances, our authority will be compromised. How can a Holy Ghost Pastor walk into a bank and beg for money to build a church building? That's not God's plan. He said we are to be the lender and not the borrower.

Trusting in God means knowing His promises for us are true and good. Not one word of God shall be void of power. God watches over His Word to perform it.[1] Because God has made this promise, we can be confident that it will always come to pass. It doesn't matter how you feel. The Scripture doesn't say, let the weak become strong and then confirm they're strong. No, rather, while they were still weak, they confessed that they were strong! You could apply that to other things as well.

Let the sick say they are healed. Let the poor say they are rich. Don't undo it by saying, "Oh, I still feel sick; it didn't work." Healing is part of your redemption in Christ. Sickness is part of the curse of the law. This doesn't mean that you pretend you aren't sick. It means you must confess your covenant, regardless of how you feel in your physical body.

> But if you ignore the LORD your God and are not careful to keep all his commandments and statutes I am giving you today, then all these curses will come upon you in full force. The LORD will plague you with deadly diseases [...]
>
> — Deuteronomy 28:15, 21 (NET)

One area that I struggled with was finances. I spent so much of my adult life living in lack that I got used to it. I got used to saying, "I can't afford it; it's too expensive; I never have enough." But I was uninformed regarding what God says about money. Mainly because, growing up in church, I usually heard a negative connotation associated with money.

I needed a fresh revelation on the subject of finances, tithes, and offerings. Learning the Biblical view of money was life-changing for me. Below I quote 4 points from a live broadcast by Evangelist Jonathan Shuttlesworth about tithing:

1. God's will is not for your life to be hard. God wants you blessed.

> All these blessings will come on you and accompany you if you obey the LORD your God: You will be blessed in the city and blessed in the country. The fruit of your womb will be blessed, and the crops of your land and the young of your livestock—the calves of your herds and the lambs of your flocks. Your basket and your kneading trough will be blessed.
>
> — Deuteronomy 28:2-5

I remember hearing certain blessings and promises were only for the Israelites but not for us today. Galatians 3:29 (NLT) corrected my understanding:

> And now that you belong to Christ, you are the true children of Abraham. You are his heirs, and God's promise to Abraham belongs to you.
>
> — Galatians 3:29 (NLT)

2. God's Word speaks blessings over you.

> The LORD will send a blessing on your barns and on everything you put your hand to. The LORD your God will bless you in the land he is giving you. The Lord will grant you abundant prosperity —in the fruit of your womb, the young of your livestock and the crops of your ground—in the land he swore to your ancestors to give you. The LORD will open the heavens, the storehouse of

> his bounty, to send rain on your land in season and to bless all the work of your hands. You will lend to many nations but will borrow from none.
>
> — Deuteronomy 28:8, 11-12

3. That blessing includes money.

> But remember the LORD your God, for it is he who gives you the ability to produce wealth, and so confirms his covenant, which he swore to your ancestors, as it is today.
>
> — Deuteronomy 8:18

For some reason, Christians hate hearing teaching about money. Like it or not, money is important. Would you rather it be in the hands of the wicked or the hands of the righteous?

4. Tithing ensures that you will lend only and never borrow.

> The LORD your God will bless you as he has promised. You will lend money to many nations but will never need to borrow. You will rule many nations, but they will not rule over you.
>
> — Deuteronomy 15:6 (NLT)

Money is not the root of all evil; the love of money is the root of all evil. Money isn't good or bad; it depends on the hands using it. The Bible makes that statement in 1 Timothy 6:10. I had to shed my belief that living with little was somehow godlier than living with abundance. Jesus was not poor; He needed a treasurer to care for his money. Jesus didn't have needs; he met needs.

Victory Over Fear, Sickness, and Defeat

> Since Judas had charge of the money, some thought
> Jesus was telling him to buy what was needed for
> the festival, or to give something to the poor.
>
> — John 13:29

Paul was persecuted for preaching the gospel, but the last thing we read about him in the book of Acts is that he rented a house for two years with enough room for people to stay with him. That doesn't sound like he was lacking in finances.

> For two whole years Paul stayed there in his own
> rented house and welcomed all who came to
> see him.
>
> — Acts 28:30

Prosperity is not simply about God meeting your needs; it's about Him blessing you abundantly so you can meet the needs of others. God wants us to prosper; that's why we're given the command to tithe. Religion doesn't accept the idea that God wants us to be rich.

> "Bring the whole tithe into the storehouse, that there
> may be food in my house. Test me in this," says
> the LORD Almighty, "and see if I will not throw
> open the floodgates of heaven and pour out so
> much blessing that there will not be room enough
> to store it."
>
> — Malachi 3:10

Tithing is not merely an "Old Testament" directive. Jesus acknowledged the need for tithing (read Matthew 23:23). There's a fantastic discourse in Hebrews Chapter 7 that discusses why tithing is a continual command. Abraham tithed to Melchizedek, which is different from the Levitical code regarding tithing.

> This man, however, did not trace his descent from
> Levi, yet he collected a tenth from Abraham and
> blessed him who had the promises.
>
> — Hebrews 7:6

> Without father or mother, without genealogy,
> without beginning of days or end of life, resem-
> bling the Son of God, he remains a priest forever.
>
> — Hebrews 7:3

Once I understood all the truths in God's Word regarding money, I couldn't speak the same way I did in the past; I had to change my vocabulary. I will never be broke another day in my life! I will not lack! I will be the lender and never the borrower! I am above and never beneath! I am the head, not the tail! (Reference: Deuteronomy 28:13)

Stop saying something is too expensive; if you don't have the finances, say, "I'll be back for it later." Don't say out loud that you won't be able to afford to pay your bills because of inflation. That's the opposite of what the Bible says.

> And my God will supply every need of yours
> according to his riches in glory in Christ Jesus.
>
> — Philippians 4:19 (ESV)

> God owns the cattle on a thousand hills (Psalm
> 50:10), so is there not enough to provide for you?
> "Look at the birds of the air; they do not sow or

reap or store away in barns, and yet your heavenly Father feeds them. Are you not much more valuable than they?"

— Matthew 6:26

And God is able to make all grace [every favor and earthly blessing] come in abundance to you, so that you may always [under all circumstances, regardless of the need] have complete sufficiency in everything [being completely self-sufficient in Him], and have an abundance for every good work and act of charity.

— 2 Corinthians 9:8 (AMP)

You won't have "just enough." You'll have more than enough because God is the God of more than enough!

---

[1] John Osteen, There's a miracle in your mouth (Houston, TX: John Osteen, 1972), 5

Chapter Sixteen

Is God in Control?

I remember one of my professors at Bible College stating, "God is not in control." My back stiffened. What kind of blasphemy was that? Fast forward to now, and my favorite Evangelist said the same thing in one of his broadcasts. I've come to realize that they're right.

The first thing you may point out is the Bible says God is sovereign. Absolutely! However, the Hebrew definition of sovereign means God is "in charge." The English definition is "a supreme ruler, possessing ultimate power." God is the Supreme Being who has all the power and oversees everything, but that doesn't mean He controls every move people make.

> We know that we are children of God and that the world around us is under the control of the evil one.
>
> — 1 John 5:19 (NLT)

> When God created mankind, He gave dominion over the earth to them.
> "[...] fill the earth and subdue it, and have dominion over the fish of the sea and over the birds of the heavens and over every living thing that moves on the earth."
>
> — Genesis 1:28 (ESV)

> The highest heavens belong to the LORD, but the earth he has given to mankind.
>
> — Psalm 115:16

> The time for judging this world has come, when Satan, the ruler of this world, will be cast out.
>
> — John 12:31 (NLT)

> Satan, who is the god of this world, has blinded the minds of those who don't believe [...]
>
> — 2 Corinthians 4:4 (NLT)

> You used to live in sin, just like the rest of the world, obeying the devil—the commander of the powers in the unseen world. He is the spirit at work in the hearts of those who refuse to obey God.
>
> — Ephesians 2:2 (NLT)

The unbelieving world is under the Devil's rule, and yes, that often includes government powers. They have a veil over their eyes; they unwittingly carry out their plans through lies and deception. But the devil doesn't have carte blanche to do what he wants. This is the hour of the church of the Lord Jesus Christ!

> Then they will come to their senses and escape from the devil's trap. For they have been held captive by him to do whatever he wants.
>
> — 2 Timothy 2:26 (NLT)

God created man to have dominion. Most preachers won't teach you that. God created man in His image. If you see a god with three arms and two heads, that's how you know you're looking at a false god. God created man to dominate. When sin entered the picture, the natural order was disrupted. Adam gave dominion over the earth to Satan. But that all changed when Jesus triumphed over Satan on the cross and took back the keys.

> [...] "Fear not, I am the first and the last, and the living one. I died, and behold I am alive forevermore, and I have the keys of Death and Hades."
>
> — Revelation 1:17-18 (ESV)

Through the death and resurrection of Jesus Christ, all dominion over the Devil has been taken back! But since Jesus returned to Heaven, what happened to that authority? He gave it to his body, the church!

> "And I will give you the keys of the Kingdom of Heaven. Whatever you forbid on earth will be forbidden in heaven, and whatever you permit on earth will be permitted in heaven."
>
> — Matthew 16:19 (NLT)

Jesus said this to Simon Peter, but it wasn't meant for him only, for the same power is promised to all believers. Keys are a symbol of authority; power to do the works of Christ.[1]

As believers, we are no longer captive to the Devil's lies.

> He has delivered us from the domain of darkness and transferred us to the kingdom of His beloved Son.
>
> — Colossians 1:13 (ESV)

Does this mean we are to sit back and let evil conquer?

Christians say that God is in control in a sense that provides comfort. But the implications of that being true, is anything but comforting. Whoever controls this world is responsible for the horrible things that happen in it. If God is loving, shouldn't He wield His control to improve things?

Why would God promise to care for us during difficult times if He was responsible for the difficulties? Just because God allows things to happen doesn't mean it is His will. Why did Jesus instruct us to pray for God's will to be done on earth as it is in Heaven if His will is already being played out on earth?

> "[...] I have set before you life and death, the blessing and the curse. So choose life in order that you may live, you and your descendants."
>
> — Deuteronomy 30:19 (NASB1995)

Satan may be the god of this world, but he doesn't have the ultimate authority. There are two agendas placed before humans to choose from, God's and Satan's. Unbelievers choose Satan's agenda through pride, ignorance, deception, or even apathy. Remember when Satan tried to tempt Jesus with the promise of power?

> Again, the devil *took Him along to a very high mountain and *showed Him all the kingdoms of the world and their glory; and he said to Him, "All these things I will give You, if You fall down and worship me."
>
> — Matthew 4:8-9 (NASB)

God doesn't force anyone to do anything. Free will was on this planet before sin.

> Then Jesus came to them and said, "All authority in heaven and on earth has been given to me."
>
> — Matthew 28:18

> [...] That power is the same as the mighty strength he exerted when he raised Christ from the dead and seated him at his right hand in the heavenly realms, far above all rule and authority, power and dominion [...]
>
> — Ephesians 1:19-21

> For in Christ all the fullness of the Deity lives in bodily form, and in Christ you have been brought to fullness. He is the head over every power and authority.
>
> — Colossians 2:9-10

Marcy Di Michele

> "Very truly I tell you, whoever believes in me will do the works I have been doing, and they will do even greater things than these, because I am going to the Father. And I will do whatever you ask in my name, so that the Father may be glorified in the Son. You may ask me for anything in my name, and I will do it."
>
> — John 14:12-14

Understand what God's will is.

> [...] he does not want anyone to be destroyed, but wants all to turn away from their sins.
>
> — 2 Peter 3:9 (GNT)

A mandate has been given to the church; many Christians often reject the concept of human responsibility.

> Then I heard the voice of the Lord saying, "Whom shall I send? And who will go for us?" And I said, "Here am I. Send me!" He said, "Go and tell this people. [...]"
>
> — Isaiah 6:8-9

God uses people to carry out His will on the earth, and it's a great commission. There's a reason why the Anti-Christ can't come into power until the church is out of the way. We carry the power of God inside of us, and our mere presence in a nation spares it from judgment. God would have spared Sodom and Gomorrah if just ten righteous people lived there (Genesis 18:32).

We are tasked with carrying out God's will on this earth. The Bible calls us the restrainer of lawlessness.

> For the secret power of lawlessness is already at work; but the one who now holds it back will continue to do so till he is taken out of the way.
>
> — 2 Thessalonians 2:7

Jesus had a limited ministry on earth; therefore, He gave a mission to His followers. The entirety of the church age sees Christians continuing that ministry.

> He said to them, "Go into all the world and preach the gospel to all creation. Whoever believes and is baptized will be saved, but whoever does not believe will be condemned. And these signs will accompany those who believe: In my name, they will drive out demons; they will speak in new tongues; they will pick up snakes with their hands; and when they drink deadly poison, it will not hurt them at all; they will place their hands on sick people, and they will get well."
>
> — Mark 16:15-18

All of this depends upon our submission to Christ. We must die to self and live for Jesus. God directs the steps of the righteous; God protects those who take refuge in Him. If we seek after God, we are hidden under the shadow of His wings. Therefore we can be confident in knowing that God has the victory, and we are on the winning side.

> "But you will receive power when the Holy Spirit comes on you, and you will be my witnesses in Jerusalem, and in all Judea and Samaria, and to the ends of the earth."
>
> — Acts 1:8

The same authority Jesus used to rebuke the wind and the waves, making them cease, lives in us.

> "However, this kind does not go out except by prayer and fasting."
>
> — Matthew 17:21 (NKJV)

God is not finished moving on this earth; He still has the ultimate power. We hear negative reports and bleak outlooks on the news, but we're not finished if the church is still here. Our job isn't complete until we hear that trumpet sound and see Jesus in the clouds.

Of course, it's easy to say God's in control. It sounds spiritual while also abdicating us of any responsibility. If God controls everything, it wouldn't matter what we did or didn't do. It wouldn't matter what we said or didn't say; our words would hold no value. That's why it's so important to understand the powerful truth about how God operates. He not only gives us free will to choose, but He also gives us an assignment.

> So he said he would destroy them—had not Moses, his chosen one, stood in the breach before him to keep his wrath from destroying them.
>
> — Psalm 106:23

> "I searched for a man among them who would build
> up the wall and stand in the gap before Me for
> [the sake of] the land, that I would not destroy it,
> but I found no one [not even one]."
>
> — Ezekiel 22:30 (AMP)

God could do everything Himself, but He chooses to equip us with His power to carry out the mission. That's an incredible privilege. God strengthens us to do the job. We know we can do nothing on our own, but nothing will be impossible with God.

> For the eyes of the LORD run to and fro throughout
> the whole earth, to give strong support to those
> whose heart is blameless toward him. [...]
>
> — 2 Chronicles 16:9 (ESV)

---

[1] Finis Jennings Dake, Dake's Annotated Reference Bible (Lawrenceville, GA: Dake Publishing Inc, 2014), 31

Chapter Seventeen

A Better Covenant

> For this reason He is the mediator of a new covenant, so that, since a death has taken place for the redemption of the violations that were committed under the first covenant, those who have been called may receive the promise of the eternal inheritance.
>
> — Hebrews 9:15 (NASB)

> But now He has obtained a more excellent ministry, to the extent that He is also the mediator of a better covenant, which has been enacted on better promises.
>
> — Hebrews 8:6 (NASB)

We know that Job lived under a different covenant, so we can't compare his situation to ours. Job lived righteous and pure, he feared God and lived in obedience, yet God allowed the Devil to attack him. That wouldn't happen to us today because we are under the blood of Christ; even Job recognized that had there been a mediator, he wouldn't have faced such trials.

> "If only there were someone to mediate between us, someone to bring us together."
>
> — Job 9:33

Nevertheless, we must be careful about how we apply the book of Job to our own lives. There is so much truth to be learned; for example, a speech given by one of Job's friends, Eliphaz the Temanite, in chapter 22. Although he was mistaken in claiming that Job had sinned and thus required repentance, the instruction still had the truth. If we break down part of his discourse, we can glean some essential advice that is very much applicable today.

> "Submit to God and be at peace with him; in this way prosperity will come to you."
>
> — Job 22:21

Other versions use the word 'acquaint' rather than 'submit'. The original language defines that word as "to be familiar with, to be serviceable to, to know intimately.[1]

Because of our reconciliation through Jesus, we are intimately acquainted with God at a deeper level than Job could have been. We can know His heart, know His nature, love what He loves, and know His voice; when we cultivate that kind of relationship with God, the second part of the verse will come to pass, and prosperity will come to us.

> "Accept instruction from his mouth and lay up his words in your heart."
>
> —Job 22:22

Obedience to God's Word, following His voice, submitting to His will, and genuinely believing what's right in your heart are the keys to supernatural success in your life. It's not wishful thinking; it's real because it's the truth according to the Word of God.

> "Surely then you will find delight in the Almighty and will lift up your face to God. You will pray to him, and he will hear you, and you will fulfil your vows."
>
> —Job 22:26-27

This Scripture reminds me a lot of Psalm 91:1, which is one of the most powerful Psalms in the entire Bible:

> Whoever dwells in the shelter of the Most High will rest in the shadow of the Almighty." There is safety, protection and blessing when we rest, submit and delight in the Lord.
>
> — Psalm 91:1

What promises can we claim if we make God our refuge?

> If you say, "The LORD is my refuge," and you make the Most High your dwelling, no harm will overtake you, no disaster will come near your tent.
>
> — Psalm 91:9-10

Marcy Di Michele

Verses 3-7 show us that:

> Surely he will save you from the fowler's snare and from the deadly pestilence. He will cover you with his feathers, and under his wings you will find refuge; his faithfulness will be your shield and rampart. You will not fear the terror of night, nor the arrow that flies by day, nor the pestilence that stalks in the darkness, nor the plague that destroys at midday. A thousand may fall at your side, ten thousand at your right hand, but it will not come near you.
>
> — Psalm 91:3-7

Verses 11-12 continue this promise, stating:

> For he will command his angels concerning you to guard you in all your ways; they will lift you up in their hands, so that you will not strike your foot against a stone.
>
> — Psalm 91:11-12

Ending this Psalm with verses 15-16, saying:

> He will call on me, and I will answer him; I will be with him in trouble, I will deliver him and honor him. With long life I will satisfy him and show him my salvation.
>
> — Psalm 91:15-16

Why should I fear death? With long life, He will satisfy me! Why should I fear sickness? No harm will overtake me; no plague is allowed near my dwelling. Why should I fear disaster? Guardian angels surround me. Why should I be afraid? I'm covered by His wings.

> The LORD is my strength and my shield; my heart trusts in him, and he helps me. My heart leaps for joy, and with my song I praise him.
>
> — Psalm 28:7

> The name of the LORD is a strong tower; the righteous man runs into it and is safe.
>
> — Proverbs 18:10 (ESV)

My God is a strong tower; He's my strength and my shield; what fear can overtake me? Speak to the mountain. Speak to the giant. Speak to the fear. Speak to the wind and the waves. As we continue in Job 22, we see what we can expect when we speak something out.

> "You will also declare a thing, and it will be established for you; so light will shine on your ways."
>
> — Job 22:28 (NKJV)

Another version says, "What you decide on will be done." Many Christians don't like verses with such implications. They have the "God is in control" mentality, and passages like this call that into question. But it's nothing to be confused over. Our behavior, actions, and adherence to the will of God will result in answered prayers. Align yourself with God's Word and His will, and you can have what you say.

Marcy Di Michele

A covenant is a binding agreement between two parties. In addition, there are conditions to be met. God makes His blessing available to all, but there are conditions attached.

> Know therefore that the Lord your God is God; he is the faithful God, keeping his covenant of love to a thousand generations of those who love him and keep his commandments. If you pay attention to these laws and are careful to follow them, then the Lord your God will keep his covenant of love with you, as he swore to your ancestors.
>
> — Deuteronomy 7:9 and 12.

Holiness is a major key to receiving the promises. You can believe them until you're blue in the face, but if you're living in disobedience, you won't receive anything from the Lord.

> Therefore, since we have these promises, dear friends, let us purify ourselves from everything that contaminates body and spirit, perfecting holiness out of reverence for God.
>
> — 2 Corinthians 7:1

> You were taught, with regard to your former way of life, to put off your old self, which is being corrupted by its deceitful desires; to be made new in the attitude of your minds; and to put on the new self, created to be like God in true righteousness and holiness.
>
> — Ephesians 4:21-24

> But now that you have been set free from sin and have become slaves of God, the benefit you reap leads to holiness, and the result is eternal life.
>
> — Romans 6:22

> So now, there is no condemnation for those who belong to Christ Jesus. And because you belong to him, the power of the life-giving Spirit has freed you from the power of sin that leads to death. The law of Moses was unable to save us because of the weakness of our sinful nature. So God did what the law could not do. He sent his own Son in a body like the bodies we sinners have. And in that body, God declared an end to sin's control over us by giving his Son as a sacrifice for our sins. He did this so that the just requirement of the law would be fully satisfied for us, who no longer follow our sinful nature but instead follow the Spirit.
>
> — Romans 8:1-4 (NLT)

Holiness is not going through the motions of obeying the law. We would fall short if we tried to keep the law in our strength. However, we don't strive with our strength! Through Christ, we are changed from the inside out. We have the Spirit of God operating inside of us!

> But now, by dying to what once bound us, we have been released from the law so that we serve in the new way of the Spirit, and not in the old way of the written code.
>
> — Romans 7:6

Purification happens on the inside of you by the Spirit of God. Without the power that operates inside us, we'll always fall short of the law. True obedience through faith guarantees blessing!

> The Spirit of God, who raised Jesus from the dead, lives in you. And just as God raised Christ Jesus from the dead, he will give life to your mortal bodies by this same Spirit living within you. Therefore, dear brothers and sisters, you have no obligation to do what your sinful nature urges you to do. For if you live by its dictates, you will die. But if through the power of the Spirit you put to death the deeds of your sinful nature, you will live. For all who are led by the Spirit of God are children of God.
>
> — Romans 8:11-14 (NLT)

---

[1] "Job 22:21". Bible Hub. 2004 (https://biblehub.com/job/22-21)

Chapter Eighteen

A Good Life

Have you ever felt as if everything in your life was going wrong? Has it ever seemed like nothing worked out; everything was always negative and challenging? You constantly prayed about the same thing, but it appeared as if nothing was changing?

It's normal to have challenges in life, but it's unscriptural to be defeated. Do we elevate these challenges, and allow them to take over our lives, or do we view them in light of what the Word of God says? Of course, we don't undermine what people go through; there are difficult circumstances and situations, and I'm not trying to brush that off. But the biggest mistake we can make is comforting people in their problems rather than extending the necessary lifeline to bring them out of their problems.

Have you ever met someone who had the same problem every time you spoke to them? It seemed like years had gone by, but they were still struggling with the same issue. Sometimes we get comfortable with our issues; we want sympathy, not solutions. Maybe that's you today, you've been saddled with never-ending difficulties, and you can't seem to get your life straight.

God's Word is not a box of tissues that we recite some verses, cry over our situation, and see nothing change. Nevertheless, that's the calling card for so many Christians. We know what the Bible says, we use it as a comfort and a feeling of peace, but it does not affect the general outcome of our everyday lives. It sounds good but brings about no tangible change.

> For the word of God is living and active, sharper than any two-edged sword, piercing to the division of soul and of spirit, of joints and of marrow, and discerning the thoughts and intentions of the heart.
>
> — Hebrews 4:12 (ESV)

Unlike every other book, the Word of God is alive; it's not some historical textbook or a volume of nice sayings. It carries a power that changes lives!

> All Scripture is God-breathed and is useful for teaching, rebuking, correcting and training in righteousness, so that the servant of God may be thoroughly equipped for every good work.
>
> — 2 Timothy 3:16-17

Don't mistake a bad day for a bad life. That's not what the Word of God promises us. We recognize we have an enemy, but we also recognize that the God we serve is stronger than Satan ever will be.

> The path of the righteous is like the light of dawn, shining brighter and brighter until midday.
>
> — Proverbs 4:18 (CSB)

Surely goodness and mercy shall follow me all the days of my life, and I shall dwell in the house of the LORD forever.

— Psalm 23:6 (ESV)

But we all, with unveiled face, beholding as in a mirror the glory of the Lord, are being transformed into the same image from glory to glory, just as by the Spirit of the Lord.

— 2 Corinthians 3:18 (NKJV)

They go from strength to strength [increasing in victorious power]; each of them appears before God in Zion.

— Psalm 84:7 (AMP)

But thanks be to God, who always leads us in triumph in Christ, and through us reveals the fragrance of the knowledge of Him in every place.

— 2 Corinthians 2:14 (NASB)

We know Satan's destiny, and he's going to try to take everyone down with him. "And I heard a loud voice saying in heaven, Now is come salvation, and strength, and the kingdom of our God, and the power of his Christ: for the accuser of our brethren is cast down, which accused them before our God day and night."

— Revelation 12:10 (KJV)

Isaiah chapter 14 gives an excellent summary of Satan's mistakes and what the reaction will be when he's finally conquered once and for all.

> How you have fallen from heaven, morning star, son of the dawn! You have been cast down to the earth, you who once laid low the nations! You said in your heart, "I will ascend to the heavens; I will raise my throne above the stars of God; I will sit enthroned on the mount of assembly, on the utmost heights of Mount Zaphon. I will ascend above the tops of the clouds; I will make myself like the Most High." But you are brought down to the realm of the dead, to the depths of the pit. Those who see you stare at you, they ponder your fate: "Is this the man who shook the earth and made kingdoms tremble, the man who made the world a wilderness, who overthrew its cities and would not let his captives go home?"
>
> — Isaiah 14:12-17

We're going to look at Satan and say, "This is the one I let torture me? This is the one who made me a victim? This is the one I let boss me around?" Let's not get to that point; let's understand now that the Devil is not over our heads; he's under our feet. He's not above us; he's below us. He's not stronger than us; with God on our side, we have victory! We're under a better covenant. He's not allowed to mess with us unless we allow him to.

Often, with a topic such as this one, preachers will highlight all the good that we can have but omit the reality of repentance. God wants to bless us; He wants us to have good things; He wants us to prosper and succeed. But just as Heaven is a real place, so too is Hell. When we die, we'll go to one of those two places.

If there has never been a time in your life where you remember repenting of your sins and committing your life to Jesus, or if you once did and have since turned away from the Lord, I encourage you to pray the following prayer out loud, with faith in your heart:

> Father, I thank You for sending Your son to set me free.
> I accept Jesus as my Lord and Savior.
> I believe in my heart that He rose from the dead.
> I confess my sins and repent of all my wrongdoing.
> I will follow Jesus all the days of my life.
> Thank You that I am now saved.
> I pray this in the mighty name of Jesus, amen.

If you prayed that prayer, congratulations! You are now part of the family of God. You will never be the same again, in Jesus' name. I encourage you to find a faith-filled, Bible-believing church and connect with them by becoming part of a community of fellow believers. We weren't meant to do life on our own; God created us for a relationship, first with Him and then with others. The Bible provides the blueprint of a church community, laid out in the book of Acts.

> And all the believers met together in one place and shared everything they had. They sold their property and possessions and shared the money with those in need. They worshipped together at the Temple each day, met in homes for the Lord's Supper, and shared their meals with great joy and generosity—all the while praising God and enjoying the goodwill of all the people. And each

> day the Lord added to their fellowship those who were being saved.
>
> — Acts 2:44-47 (NLT)

There's a special anointing at the gathering of the saints, and the Bible instructs us to meet together more often, not less often!

> Not giving up meeting together, as some are in the habit of doing, but encouraging one another—and all the more as you see the Day approaching.
>
> — Hebrews 10:25

Life doesn't worsen when you get saved; you don't lament all the things you had to give up to follow Jesus. When the disciples commented to Jesus about everything they left behind, he promptly rebuked them.

> Then Peter said to him, "We've given up everything to follow you. What will we get?" Jesus replied, "I assure you that when the world is made new and the Son of Man sits upon his glorious throne, you who have been my followers will also sit on twelve thrones, judging the twelve tribes of Israel. And everyone who has given up houses or brothers or sisters or father or mother or children or property, for my sake, will receive a hundred times as much in return and will inherit eternal life.
>
> — Matthew 19:27-29 (NLT)

Every day with Jesus is better than the day before. I am going from glory to glory, strength to strength, and victory to victory. I am not the same as I used to be! My life is on a different track.

Pray this aloud. Declare it!

Father, I thank You for Your great blessings. I give You all the praise and the glory and the honor, for You are great and greatly to be praised. There is none like You, no one besides You, no one above You. I am never on my own; You go before me, behind me, and beside me. What a joy it is to know that I am never alone. I have the power of Your Spirit operating inside of me. What a glorious hope to know that I am secure in Your love, in this life, and in the life to come. I am blessed beyond measure; I am blessed to overflowing.

The last defeat I had will be the last defeat I ever have! I am victorious because Jesus triumphed over Satan. The Devil is not over my head; he is under my feet. I'm not worried about him; rather, he's worried about me!

I will make a difference on this earth for the Kingdom of God. I now know that my mission is to transfer those living in darkness into the Kingdom of Your glorious light. No weapon formed against me will prosper. If God is for me, who then can be against me?

Thank You, Father, for sending Jesus. Thank You for the name that is above every other name; demons have to flee at the mention of that name. I never have to worry or be afraid. My name is written in the Lamb's book of life. My covenant is in Heaven. I am more than a conqueror through Christ. I'm a winner because You've already won. In Jesus' name, amen.

Afterword

In 2004, while attending my first semester at Bible College, God spoke to my spirit that I was supposed to write a book. I had always loved to write; as a child, I won awards for my creative writing; in high school, I had a short story published; as an adult, I became a sports journalist and even ghostwrote a book. Throughout the years, I had ideas for books, but I never had peace with any of those topics. I did manage to finish one and even sent the manuscript to a publishing contest, but it wasn't meant to be.

Eighteen years after that instruction from the Lord, the right idea dropped into my spirit, and the words just flowed out of me. My goal for this book is that it will be a resource of knowledge and that through my testimony, you'll be encouraged to seek the Lord freshly.

I want my life to glorify God, I want my life to reflect God's promises, and I want my life to please Him. I want to live according to His statutes, walk in His ways and get everything I can out of God's Word.

Afterword

My prayer is that your understanding has deepened while reading the pages of this book, and your faith will grow in strength. And if you see a verse more than once and wonder why it's there again, that's because it needs to be drilled into your heart and mind so you never forget it!

> So then faith cometh by hearing and hearing by the word of God.
>
> — Romans 10:17 (KJV)

Hear Scripture, listen to the truth of God's Word, speak His promises out loud, and you will build up your faith. The more you repeat Scripture, and the more it's spoken out, the stronger your faith becomes. When you constantly repeat that truth, it becomes very difficult to forget. An intimate relationship with God and His Word is the key to understanding His nature, and His will.

When you loose the Word of God from your mouth, you're unleashing the sword of the Spirit, and the Devil can't do anything about it. In the Old Testament, God's people had to do everything physically; they had to put their foot on the physical ground so they could take the land. As New Testament believers, our words are the way we put our feet on the ground. We speak out the promises of God to possess them.

The land of Canaan is a type of promise which God has given to believers. You were once in bondage from sin (Egypt), but God broke you out (redemption through Christ), and now there are promises available for you to receive.

It's difficult to be discouraged when you're constantly ingesting the Word of God, speaking it out, and repeating it over and over. Fill your heart and mind with sound doctrine and sound preaching, and your words will reflect that. It's hard to speak words of death when

Afterword

you're full of the joy of the Lord. We confess the promises of God and know in our hearts that God will watch over His Word and make it good.[1]

> Then the Lord said to me, "You have seen well, for I am watching over my word to perform it."
>
> —Jeremiah 1:12 (ESV)

The miracle is in your mouth; dare to speak those promises out loud. Say them to yourself; say them to the Devil; say them to the sickness; say them to the mountain. Confess them in the face of all contrary evidence.[2] Where are the promises found? In the Word of God: read it, memorize it, speak it! The Devil can't read your thoughts, but he can hear the words you speak.

He cannot overcome a child of God who knows their covenant and knows what is theirs through Christ. He can't overcome a Christian who speaks the right way!

If you read a verse once and never look at it again, there may not be much of an impact. But if you constantly repeat it, read it over and over, and let it sink deep into your spirit, it will come alive inside you. Have you ever read a Bible story that you've heard dozens of times, but now you notice something new, something you hadn't seen before? That's because it's alive; it speaks to your spirit. That's why you shouldn't only read the Bible once and never pick it up again.

I pray that you allow the Holy Spirit to be your guide and prayerfully consider everything that you read in the pages of this book. God is for you, and if God is for you, no one can be against you!

> When the Spirit of truth comes, he will guide you into all the truth, for he will not speak on his own

Afterword

> authority, but whatever he hears he will speak, and he will declare to you the things that are to come.
>
> — John 16:13 (ESV)

---

[1] John Osteen, There's a miracle in your mouth (Houston, TX: John Osteen, 1972), 27

[2] John Osteen, There's a miracle in your mouth (Houston, TX: John Osteen, 1972), 6

Memory Verses

Peace and hope:

> Do not be anxious about anything, but in everything by prayer and supplication with thanksgiving let your requests be made known to God. And the peace of God, which surpasses all understanding, will guard your hearts and your minds in Christ Jesus.
>
> — Philippians 4:6-7 (ESV)

> Humble yourselves, therefore, under the mighty hand of God so that at the proper time he may exalt you, casting all your anxieties on him, because he cares for you.
>
> — 1 Peter 5:6-7 (ESV)

Memory Verses

Cast your burden upon the LORD and He will sustain you; He will never allow the righteous to be shaken.

— Psalm 55:22 (NASB)

When my anxious thoughts multiply within me, Your comfort delights my soul.

— Psalm 94:19 (NASB)

"Therefore I tell you, do not worry about your life, what you will eat or drink; or about your body, what you will wear. Is not life more than food, and the body more than clothes? Look at the birds of the air; they do not sow or reap or store away in barns, and yet your heavenly Father feeds them. Are you not much more valuable than they? Can any one of you by worrying add a single hour to your life?"

— Matthew 6:25-27

Peace I leave with you; my peace I give to you. Not as the world gives do I give to you. Let not your hearts be troubled, neither let them be afraid.

— John 14:27 (ESV)

Do not let your hearts be troubled. You believe in God; believe also in me.

— John 14:1

Do not fear:

> For God gave us a spirit not of fear but of power and love and self-control.
>
> — 2 Timothy 1:7 (ESV)

> Have I not commanded you? Be strong and courageous. Do not be frightened, and do not be dismayed, for the Lord your God is with you wherever you go.
>
> — Joshua 1:9 (ESV)

> So we can confidently say, "The Lord is my helper; I will not fear; what can man do to me?"
>
> — Hebrews 13:6 (ESV)

> When I am afraid, I put my trust in you. In God, whose word I praise—in God I trust and am not afraid. What can mere mortals do to me?
>
> — Psalm 56:3-4

> I sought the Lord, and he answered me; he delivered me from all my fears.
>
> — Psalm 34:4

> But now, this is what the Lord says—he who created you, Jacob, he who formed you, Israel:

Memory Verses

"Do not fear, for I have redeemed you; I have summoned you by name; you are mine. When you pass through the waters, I will be with you, and when you pass through the rivers, they will not sweep over you. When you walk through the fire, you will not be burned; the flames will not set you ablaze.

— Isaiah 43:1-2

Promises of protection:

If you say, "The Lord is my refuge," and you make the Most High your dwelling, no harm will overtake you, no disaster will come near your tent.

— Psalm 91:9-10

The name of the LORD is a strong tower; The righteous runs into it and is safe.

— Proverbs 18:10 (NASB)

No weapon formed against you shall prosper, And every tongue which rises against you in judgment You shall condemn. This is the heritage of the servants of the LORD, And their righteousness is from Me," Says the LORD.

— Isaiah 54:17 (NKJV)

What, then, shall we say in response to these things? If God is for us, who can be against us?

— Romans 8:31

The Lord will keep you from all harm—he will watch over your life; the Lord will watch over your coming and going both now and forevermore.

— Psalm 121:7-8

The Lord will rescue me from every evil attack and will bring me safely to his heavenly kingdom. To him be glory for ever and ever. Amen.

— 2 Timothy 4:18

Promises of prosperity:

And this same God who takes care of me will supply all your needs from his glorious riches, which have been given to us in Christ Jesus.

— Philippians 4:19 (NLT)

Honor the Lord with your wealth and with the first fruits of all your produce; then your barns will be filled with plenty, and your vats will be bursting with wine.

— Proverbs 3:9-10 (ESV)

Oh, taste and see that the Lord is good! Blessed is the man who takes refuge in him! Oh, fear the Lord, you his saints, for those who fear him have no lack! The young lions suffer want and hunger; but those who seek the Lord lack no good thing.

— Psalm 34:8-10 (ESV)

The thief does not come except to steal, and to kill, and to destroy. I have come that they may have life, and that they may have it more abundantly.

— John 10:10 (NKJV)

And you shall again obey the voice of the Lord and keep all his commandments that I command you today. The Lord your God will make you abundantly prosperous in all the work of your hand, in the fruit of your womb and in the fruit of your cattle and in the fruit of your ground. For the Lord will again take delight in prospering you, as he took delight in your fathers, when you obey the voice of the Lord your God, to keep his commandments and his statutes that are written in this Book of the Law, when you turn to the Lord your God with all your heart and with all your soul.

— Deuteronomy 30:8-10 (ESV)

Let them shout for joy and be glad, who favor my righteous cause. And let them say continually "Let the Lord be magnified, Who has pleasure in the prosperity of His servant".

— Psalm 35:27 (NKJV)

According as his divine power hath given unto us all things that pertain unto life and godliness, through the knowledge of him that hath called us to glory and virtue.

— 2 Peter 1:3 (KJV)

Promises of health:

Worship the Lord your God, and his blessing will be on your food and water. I will take away sickness from among you.

— Exodus 23:25

Is anyone among you sick? Let them call the elders of the church to pray over them and anoint them with oil in the name of the Lord. 15 And the prayer offered in faith will make the sick person well; the Lord will raise them up. If they have sinned, they will be forgiven.

— James 5:14-15

Praise the Lord, my soul, and forget not all his benefits—who forgives all your sins and heals all your diseases, who redeems your life from the pit and crowns you with love and compassion, who satisfies your desires with good things so that your youth is renewed like the eagle's.

— Psalm 103:2-5

Memory Verses

How God anointed Jesus of Nazareth with the Holy Spirit and power, and how he went around doing good and healing all who were under the power of the Devil, because God was with him.

— Acts 10:38

That evening they brought to him many who were oppressed by demons, and he cast out the spirits with a word and healed all who were sick. This was to fulfill what was spoken by the prophet Isaiah: "He took our illnesses and bore our diseases."

— Matthew 8:16-17

He said, "If you listen carefully to the Lord your God and do what is right in his eyes, if you pay attention to his commands and keep all his decrees, I will not bring on you any of the diseases I brought on the Egyptians, for I am the Lord, who heals you."

— Exodus 15:26

Surely he will save you from the fowler's snare and from the deadly pestilence. He will cover you with his feathers, and under his wings you will find refuge; his faithfulness will be your shield and rampart. You will not fear the terror of night, nor the arrow that flies by day, nor the pestilence that stalks in the darkness, nor the plague that destroys at midday. A thousand may fall at your

Memory Verses

side, ten thousand at your right hand, but it will not come near you.

— Psalm 91:3-7

Acknowledgments

Special thanks to my editor, Lisa, and my photographer, Anthony.

To my husband, thank you for your never-ending love and support.

To my parents, for being the greatest examples of life and godliness.

To my best friend, for always being there.

To my Pastors, thank you for believing in me.

Thanks Evangelist Jonathan, for being an inspiration.

And to the Mondays with Marcy family, you are the best.

I love you all.

But most importantly, all the glory to God for giving me the ability to write, and the anointing to communicate His truth.

About the Author

Marcy felt the call into the ministry when she was 16 years old. After earning a degree in music at a secular college, she went to Bible School in Australia and graduated from Hillsong International Leadership College in 2005. She then took a position as a Youth Pastor at a church in Ontario.

In 2013, Marcy took a position at a new church plant in Ontario as a Music and Youth Pastor, and there she was ordained into the ministry.

She now teaches in a Bible School, preaches, and has a weekly live broadcast, and podcast.

In fulfilling her calling, Marcy's ministry and testimony have impacted countless lives. She continues to build faith in others by teaching the Word, sharing the gospel, and encouraging people through God's promises.

Marcy has been married to her husband David, since 2005.

Keep up to date on Marcy's ministry: www.onlymarcy.com

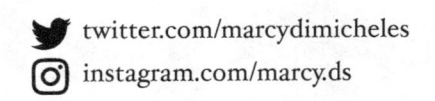

twitter.com/marcydimicheles
instagram.com/marcy.ds

CPSIA information can be obtained
at www.ICGtesting.com
Printed in the USA
BVHW070239261122
652778BV00004B/786